Endorsements

"If you are plagued by an eating disorder, read and work through this study guide. If you are not plagued by an eating disorder, read and work through this study guide. It's really for anyone who wants to grow in grace and holiness. Jennifer Lane is a wise, compassionate, and battle-hardened pilgrim who points the way to emotional, physical, and spiritual health through faith in Christ. You can trust her. I read it to review it. I'm reading it again to grow."

Ben Patterson, author of 12 books including *Deepening Your Conversation with God* and *Waiting: Finding Hope When God Seems Silent*

"*Transformed* is a Bible study and healing tool for disordered eating that goes to the depth of soul where true restoration and change takes place. As a therapist and overcomer of anorexia and bulimia myself, I am grateful for this biblically sound and yet practical tool for women with disordered eating. Jennifer Lane writes with excellence, caring for the body, soul, and spirit of each reader. I will recommend this Bible study to clients and women seeking wholeness for a lifetime."

Brenda L. Yoder, licensed mental health counselor, speaker, and author of *Fledge: Launching Your Kids Without Losing Your Mind*

"*Transformed* by Jennifer Smith Lane is rock solid and genuinely helpful. Born out of her own story, Jennifer writes with courageous vulnerability as she calls us to embrace renewal God's way. There are no shortcuts, magic formulas, or easy steps, but stories of authentic life change that instill hope and a path toward healing. This study uses the living and active Word of God to penetrate the lies that bind us. It is an invitation for the Lord to speak His grace and truth into our hurts, fears, and heart desires. He is the *One* who made us—body, soul and spirit—and *He* delights in freeing us from enslaving deceptions so that we might follow Him on a journey of deep and lasting transformation."

Dr. Jerry Sheveland, pastor and former president of Converge Worldwide

"This book has truly been forged in prayer and years of applying God's Truth! All to help many expose the underlying spiritual issues that keep them stuck in eating and body image struggles and bring them into freedom as minds and hearts are enlightened through God's living Word. I'm excited this amazing tool is now available so that many more may experience the depth of God's love and be enabled, encouraged, and empowered to live as God designed them!"

Susan Sorensen, women's ministry director and author of several books and Bible studies including *Praying Through Cancer*

"In my own journey through my food disorder, I tried countless times to modify my behavior—eat less, exercise more. My relationship with food was based on creating a sense of safety and security, so this behavior modification alone would never actually produce long-lasting fruit. It wasn't until I dug down deep and allowed God into my heart *and* behaviors that real change began to take place. And this is what I love about this study: from the very beginning it's about your heart and a transformation that can only truly take place from the inside out."

Jen Ferguson, author of *Pure Eyes, Clean Heart: A Couple's Journey to Freedom from Pornography*

"Jen's life has truly been transformed by the power of God's Spirit. We are grateful she has written this book to help readers discover the scriptural truths and spiritual practices that allowed her to experience freedom from lies and shame."

Jim Samra, author and pastor of Calvary Church, Grand Rapids, MI
Lisa Samra, author and editor

Transformed

Eating and Body Image Renewal God's Way

JENNIFER SMITH LANE

Readers should be aware that Internet Web sites mentioned as references or sources for further information may have changed or no longer be available since this book was published.

Published by Jennifer Smith Lane

ISBN (Softcover Trade Edition) 978-1-7334085-0-9

Scripture quotations marked (ESV) are taken from the ESV® Bible (The Holy Bible, English Standard Version®). ESV® Text Edition: 2016. Copyright © 2001 by Crossway, a publishing ministry of Good News Publishers. The ESV® text has been reproduced in cooperation with and by permission of Good News Publishers. Unauthorized reproduction of this publication is prohibited. All rights reserved.

Scripture quotations marked (ISV) are taken from the Holy Bible: International Standard Version. Release 2.0, Build 2015.02.09. Copyright © 1995-2014 by ISV Foundation. ALL RIGHTS RESERVED INTERNATIONALLY. Used by permission of Davidson Press, LLC.

Scripture quotations marked (NASB) are taken from the NEW AMERICAN STANDARD BIBLE®, Copyright © 1960, 1962, 1963, 1968, 1971, 1972, 1973, 1975, 1977, 1995 by The Lockman Foundation. Used by permission.

Scripture quotations marked (NIV) are taken from THE HOLY BIBLE, NEW INTERNATIONAL VERSION®, NIV® Copyright © 1973, 1978, 1984, 2011 by Biblica, Inc.® Used by permission. All rights reserved worldwide.

Scripture quotations marked (NKJV) are taken from the New King James Version.® Copyright © 1982 by Thomas Nelson. Used by permission. All rights reserved.

Scripture quotations marked (NLT) are taken from the Holy Bible, New Living Translation, copyright © 1996, 2004, 2007 by Tyndale House Foundation. Used by permission of Tyndale House Publishers, Inc., Carol Stream, Illinois 60188. All rights reserved.

Scripture quotations marked (TPT) are from The Passion Translation.® Copyright © 2017, 2018 by Passion & Fire Ministries, Inc. Used by permission. All rights reserved. ThePassionTranslation.com.

Editor: Kathy Bruins

Cover design: Michael Sean Allen

Interior Art and Layout Design: James Armstrong

Free vector graphics by vecteezy.com

Trade distribution is provided by the IngramSpark.®
To purchase this book for trade distribution, go to www.ingramspark.com.

For media requests and interviews, go to www.JenniferSmithLane.com

Printed in the USA
May 2020 Version

Contents

Dear Fellow Sojourner,

God's journey for me has taken me down many paths that I was not expecting. As these twists and turns came, so did feelings of rejection, abandonment, failure, fear, and shame. The fairy tale story I had always dreamed about wasn't coming true, and I believed the lie that I was powerless to change the ending. The crushing weight of intense stress, anxiety, and emotions caused me to find rescue in the counterfeit arms of an eating disorder; my pride was keeping me from asking for any help. Now, deeply entrenched, the eating disorder betrayed me. It didn't rescue me but enslaved me, and I found myself fighting for my life. Despite seven years of various kinds of top-notch treatment, I couldn't break free, and finally resigned myself to live the rest of my life ensnared. However, in my complete brokenness, hopelessness and desperation, God intervened and showed me the lies I believed about myself that kept me powerless and captive. Confessing those lies and turning them over to God brought newfound freedom into my life. Today, I walk free of eating and body image issues. Beloved, there is hope for your freedom too.

Freedom did not come overnight; rather it came through a slow transformative process within my heart. I desperately wanted a checklist to follow from my treatment team, believing marking off completed tasks would bring me the healing and freedom I longed for. But what I discovered is that the healing path wasn't orderly, but messy. Much of the time I felt no progress was being made. Healing is hard. But God changed my perspective and gave me a new pair of lenses to see my situation more clearly. Instead of asking God, "Why is this happening to me?" He challenged me to ask Him, "What are you teaching me through this?"

The new lenses helped me believe the truth instead of lies. God was inviting me to surrender my will to Him, trust Him, and walk with Him on the path He designed for me. But how could I commit to walk with Him when I had no idea of the outcome? My perfectionistic, controlling self didn't respond well to this thought. In that moment, God reminded me that He promises to never leave me or forsake me, that He is a faithful, loving and sovereign God whom I can trust. He didn't ask me or expect me to change in an instant; instead, He asked me to just take one step towards Him. To say I was hesitant would be an understatement. When I finally took that step of faith with Him, it started me on a journey of transformation resulting in healing and freedom far beyond what I could have asked.

Now it's your turn to answer God's call. As God exposes the dark areas in your heart, remember its not to condemn you but to set you free. With the turn of each page, yield yourself to your Maker. Allow God to handle you as the potter handles the clay and so *transform [your] Valley of Trouble into a gateway of hope* (Hosea 2:15 NLT).

Warmly,
Jen

Dedication

To all who are struggling with eating and body image issues,
feeling hopeless, powerless, and alone;
I know that place...
Know that God sees you, hears you, and loves you.

"Lord, I pray You will bestow on her a crown of beauty instead of ashes,
the oil of joy instead of mourning,
and a garment of praise instead of a spirit of despair.
May she be called an oak of righteousness,
a planting of the Lord for the display of Your splendor."

adapted from Isaiah 61:3 (NIV)

TRANSFORMED – EATING AND BODY IMAGE RENEWAL GOD'S WAY

Introduction

The study is called *Transformed* because we are about to embark on a transformation journey together. A journey by definition takes you from one place to another and requires perseverance, determination, and grit on your part, but on this journey you will not be traveling alone. As you open your heart to God, He will be present to comfort, encourage, prune, lead, and ultimately transform you. Our road map comes from Romans 12:12 which says, *"Don't copy the behavior and customs of this world, but let God transform you into a new person by changing the way you think. Then you will learn to know God's will for you, which is good and pleasing and perfect"* (NLT).[1]

Each session of this study has 7 different components utilized over a 5-day span that will help you expose worldly ideals and teach you practical strategies to help change the way you think and open the door for God to transform you inside and out. Here is an overview:

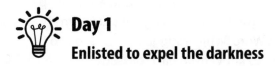

Day 1
Enlisted to expel the darkness

The word *enlisted* is a military term that describes signing up for something. When you accepted Jesus Christ* you were enlisted into God's army. Part of our assignment, Christ followers, is to be a light (Matthew 5:15-16) in the world. When you allow Christ to shine through you, it brings things once in darkness into the light.

This section is designed to expose underlying spiritual issues that may be keeping you stuck in eating and body image struggles, which I believe affects us on emotional, physical, and spiritual levels. In my experience, all three areas need to be addressed in order to achieve freedom that lasts. By inviting God into the process, you invite the Lord to do a transformative work in you, giving you total freedom that can only come from Him.

*(If you haven't accepted Jesus Christ as your personal Lord and Savior, that's OK! But there's no time like the present! Turn to the appendix and I can walk you through how to do that.)

Day 2
Entangled by sin

When you are entangled in something, it means you're ensnared, stuck, struggling to escape. That is often how it feels when you're struggling with eating and body image issues. Whether you struggle with anorexia, bulimia, binge eating, overeating, emotional eating, extreme dieting, preoccupation with healthy food, or body dissatisfaction—no matter where you fall on the spectrum of eating and body image struggles—I believe the underlying causes that keep people enslaved are universal. Often, we are unaware of how much some of these areas are fueling our disordered thinking and causing us to engage in self-harming eating behaviors. Life brings circumstances across our path that are difficult to escape. The trouble with disordered eating and body image is that you are forced to face those negative feelings about yourself every time you feel hungry. You can't decide to never eat again. Nourishment is a part of God's design. You can't avoid hunger and the slew of emotions it brings. Therefore, each session helps you prayerfully explore some of these different areas that may be keeping you stuck in your eating and body image struggles.

Day 3
Enlightened through Scripture study

Proverbs 7:1, 3b says *"…Store up my commands within you…write them on the tablet of your heart"* (NIV).[2] I can think of nothing more vital to your freedom journey than discovering the truth in God's Word and then writing it on your heart to create a firm foundation upon which to build. God has given us the gift of His Word, and it is our job to learn the many truths in it so that we can be confident of who we are in Christ. Through inductive Bible study tools*, you will learn how to observe, interpret, and apply Scripture through a systematic study of God's Word. The tools are designed to enhance your study time** as you prayerfully invite God to reveal Himself to you through His Word. While I suggest a few tools to try in each session, I encourage you to ask God what He wants you to know from each passage in order to guide and direct you in your personal walk with Him.

*An outline and more in-depth explanation of this method can be found in the appendix.
**Scripture study pages for inductive marking available for free download at jennifersmithlane.com/resources.

Day 4
Encourage through testimony

While sin appears enticing at first, it eventually leads us away from God, even enslaving us to it at times. This can be a shame-filled, hopeless, and despairing place, but know you are not alone. Twelve brave women have offered to share their eating and body image journeys with you in hopes that you might be encouraged on yours. While the names and details have been changed, their stories are real and true. Be encouraged. Be hopeful. God can make life without disordered and body image issues possible.

Day 5
Entrusted and empowered to tell others

When I was in the throes of my eating disorder, I used to beg God to use this struggle for good. While I am not proud of this part of my life, I truly believe that *"God intended it for good to accomplish what is now being done, the saving of many lives"* (Genesis 50:20 NIV). God entrusted these truths to me during some of the darkest parts of my life, and I share them with you with joy. This section challenges you to take the new truths that you've learned and apply them to your own life and the lives of others.

Engage: Converse with God through journaling

As God shines His light and exposes things you need to work through, it often stirs up a lot of thoughts, feelings, and questions. This section of the study will appear at the end of every day to help you process all of these with the Lord. The questions are designed to be more like conversation starters to get you going in your dialog with Him.* God cares about what we are thinking and feeling, but often we don't take the time to tell Him. I hope this will foster your relationship with God as you engage Him on anything and everything.

*You may want to purchase a journal to give yourself plenty of room to dialogue with God.

Enabled through spiritual practices

To whom do you turn when you're stressed, upset, discouraged, or afraid? Do you turn to a friend, a family member, a spouse, a counselor, or a pastor, hoping that they will be your knight in shining armor and rescue you? In this section, I have provided practical ways for you to use spiritual disciplines to actively combat urges, emotions, and habits. Maybe you think "spiritual disciplines" must be for super-special, spiritual people, but they are not. They are for all of us. They consist of simple tools you can use to help you turn to God for rescue and bring you into closer communion with Him.

Appendix

Find a detailed description of the inductive method, answers to frequently asked questions, and resources for participants and leaders in the Appendix.

Thank you for your willingness to embark on this journey with me. I consider it an honor and privilege to walk with you. It is my prayer that God would do a transformative work in your heart and mind, making you more like Him with each turn of the page. May He accomplish infinitely more than you could ever ask or think (Ephesians 3:20) as you pursue Him on this journey. Glory be to God.

ENDNOTES

1   Holy Bible: New Living Translation (Wheaton, IL: Tyndale House Publishers, 2004).
2   Holy Bible: New International Version (Grand Rapids, MI: Zondervan 1984, 2011).

Transformed: From Mess to Masterpiece

Day 1
Enlisted to Expose the Darkness

Makeovers. We find story after story in magazines and on TV, featuring one lucky woman's opportunity to have "a complete makeover" of her wardrobe, her makeup, her hair, her weight, her living room, her closets. The before picture often reveals her mess, and the after picture unveils the finished masterpiece. The stark contrast between the before and after pictures stop you in your tracks. You wonder how could such a complete transformation be possible? As the story unfolds, you realize that she had all the components of a masterpiece, but she just needed some help to get there. Isn't that just like us? Don't we all need a little help in transforming our mess into a masterpiece?

What does it mean to be transformed? Transformed comes from the Greek word *metamorphoo*[1] which means to change into another form. Think of a caterpillar's dramatic metamorphic change into a butterfly. Talk about a makeover! Maybe you can understand the transformation of a butterfly but you have a hard time seeing what transformation would look like in you. Consider C. S. Lewis' description of it given in *Mere Christianity*:

> *"Imagine yourself as a living house. God comes in to rebuild that house. At first, perhaps, you can understand what He is doing. He is getting the drains right and stopping the leaks in the roof and so on; you knew that those jobs needed doing and so you are not surprised. But presently He starts knocking the house about in a way that hurts abominably and does not seem to make any sense. What on earth is He up to? The explanation is that He is building quite a different house from the one you thought of—throwing out a new wing here, putting on an extra floor there, running up towers, making courtyards. You thought you were being made into a decent little cottage: but He is building a palace. He intends to come and live in it Himself."*[2]

Friend, God wants to remodel, renovate, and make you over. Will you let Him?

Engage with God

o   Are there any parts of your life that need some renovations or a makeover?

o   What things have you tried to bring about a change?

o   Are you willing to invite God in to transform your mess into His masterpiece?

Enabled through Spiritual Practice

Self-examination invites the Holy Spirit to search your heart by opening yourself to your loving Maker as you seek transformation. You are going to work on taking your before picture snapshot so that when you reach the end of the study, you can appreciate the work that has been done to clean up your mess!

When was the last time you invited God into the conversation about how you feel about your body? I challenge you to have an honest discussion about your body with yourself and with the Lord. Stand in front of a mirror (full length if possible) and look at your body front and back. Begin by thanking God for how He designed you. As you work your way down from the top of your head to the soles of your feet, tell the Lord genuinely what you think about each part. He can handle your honesty. Then ask Him what He thinks about it and consider God's purpose in His design. Write down what He shows you and let gratitude flow freely.

Ponder these questions and record your answers:

o   How do I see myself?

o   How did thanking God for my body alter my feelings and perceptions about it?

o   Do I need to do something differently so that I am in step with my Creator's design?

o   How is God asking me to care for the body He created for me?

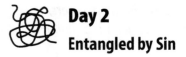 **Day 2**
Entangled by Sin

Ephesians 2:10 says, *"We are God's handiwork created in Christ Jesus to do good works which God prepared in advance for us to do"* (NIV). "God's handiwork"? What does that even mean?

"Handiwork" comes from the Greek word *poiema*[3] which gives us our English word for poem and it means, "What has been made." It can also be translated workmanship or masterpiece or creation. That means you are something made by God's hand. Have you ever considered yourself a work of divine poetry? I'm guessing probably not. Do you realize what that means? It means that when God created you, He created a masterpiece. It means you are a work of art that is one of a kind, custom designed, and tailor made by the Master's hand! Often when we look at ourselves, we don't see a masterpiece at all. Instead our view is distorted by lenses that magnify every little flaw, blemish, and imperfection like a flashing neon sign demands our attention. But that is not what God sees. Psalm 139 describes it this way

He knows when I sit and when I rise (2)

He is familiar with all my ways (3)

He is with me guiding me and holding me fast (10)

He created my inmost being (13)

He knit me together in my mother's womb (13)

His works are fearfully and wonderfully made (14)

He saw my unformed body when I was made in the secret place (15-16)

He searches me and knows my heart (23)

He leads me in the way everlasting (24)

God knows you. He knows your thoughts and actions. He's with you, guiding you, anchoring you. He created you, designed you, and you're breathtaking. He knew you from the beginning, inside and out. He loves you enough to search your heart and then lead you with an eternal purpose. In fact, God loves you so much, He sent His Son to die on the cross for you! So why do we have such a hard time accepting these truths and seeing ourselves the way God sees us?

I like how Nancy DeMoss Wolgemuth puts it in her book, *Lies Women Believe and The Truth That Sets Them Free*:

> *"It is conceivable that someone who did not recognize or appreciate fine art would toss a masterpiece into the trash. Would that make the painting any less valuable? Not at all. The true worth of the art would be seen when an art collector spotted the painting and said, "That is a priceless piece, and I am willing to pay any amount to acquire it. When God sent His Only Son, Jesus to this earth to bear your sin and mine on the cross, He put a price tag on us--He declared the value of our soul to be greater than the value of the whole world. Whose opinion are you going to accept? Believing a lie will put you in bondage. Believing Truth will set you free."*[4]

If you were standing with an artist before their masterpiece, would you point out all the things you don't like about it, what he could have done differently to make it better or brazenly take a brush to alter his work? Probably not. However, don't we do the same thing when we scoff at our bodies in front of our Maker? The prophet Isaiah says it this way, *"Shall what is formed say to the one who formed it, 'You did not make me'? Can the pot say to the potter, 'You know nothing'"* (Isaiah 29:16 NIV)? Ouch! I don't know about you, but I never thought of my sharp critiques of my body as harsh criticism of my Creator.

Even though you may not appreciate yourself as fine art and you may feel like you should just be tossed in the trash, it doesn't make you, God's creation, any less valuable! 2 Corinthians 3:5 says, *"Not that we are adequate in ourselves to consider anything as coming from ourselves, but our adequacy is from God"* (NASB).[5] The enemy will try to convince you otherwise and you may not even be able to discern the truth from lies, but don't let that stop you. Take a minute and soak in the truth that even if you did nothing to change yourself, you are enough just the way you are.

Maybe you can relate to one of the characters in one of George MacDonald's books who says, "I wonder why God made me? I certainly don't see any purpose in it!" to which another character responds, "Perhaps you don't see any purpose yet, but then, He isn't finished making you. And besides, you are arguing with the process."[6]

As we embark on our journey together, ask God to help you see yourself as He sees you and resist the temptation to argue with the process. Ask Him to remove the web of lies that are keeping you from seeing yourself for who you truly are. If you ever begin to doubt how much God loves you or how pleased He is with you as His creation, take off those old lenses and remind yourself of how God sees you:

> loved, (Ephesians 3:19)
>
> chosen, (1 Peter 2:9, Ephesians 1:4)
>
> accepted, (John 15:15-16)
>
> precious, (Isaiah 43:4a)
>
> redeemed, (Ephesians 1:7)
>
> forgiven, (Psalm 103:12)
>
> victorious, (Romans 8:37)
>
> blameless, (Romans 8:1)
>
> fearfully and wonderfully made, (Psalm 139:14)
>
> God's masterpiece! (Ephesians 2:10)

Engage with God

o   Was it hard for you to accept the idea that you are God's masterpiece, or did grasping the depths of how God knows you change anything about the way you see or think about yourself?

o   Look at the list of words above that Scripture uses to describe who you are. Which word resonated most with you and why?

o   What can you do to integrate this promise of Scripture into your daily life this week?

Enabled through Spiritual Practice

Yesterday you completed the difficult assignment of having an honest conversation with God about your body. I am proud of you! As you did the mirror exercise, I asked you to keep 1 Corinthians 6:19 at the forefront of your mind and to not lose sight that your body houses the Holy Spirit. Verse 20 goes on to say, *"You do not belong to yourself, for God bought you with a high price and you must honor God with your body"* (NLT). While using the tool of self-examination, keep this verse in mind as you reflect on how you can "honor God with your body."

Reflect on these questions and record your answers:

o   Are there any changes I need to make in regard to sleep, exercise, eating, or drinking in order to be a good steward of the body God entrusted to me?

o   Am I engaging in any harmful behaviors to my body that are not honoring to God?

o   Proverbs 4:23 says *"Guard your heart, for everything you do flows from it"* (NIV). What flows from your heart? Is there anything you need to do differently in order to guard your heart and your body?

 ## Day 3
Enlightened through Scripture Study

Pray

Lord, thank you for showing me the truth about who I am and who you created me to be. Write these truths on my heart and bring them to mind whenever my mind begins to wander away from You. Firmly plant the words of Psalm 139 in my heart today as I study so that they may take root and grow in my heart. In Jesus name I pray, Amen.

Observe

Passage: Psalm 139 (NIV)

When we ask questions, the goal is to gather more information or facts about the setting, the context, the people, and the events. For Psalm 139, try asking these questions:

o   Who is the author?
o   How often is God mentioned? (Be sure to also mark pronouns)
o   Why is LORD written in capital letters?
o   What does God know about you?

If we want to emphasize something, we often repeat the same word or phrase more than once. God does the same thing in His Word. Look for repeated words or phrases.

- o Mark all forms of the word know, including synonyms like perceive, discern, and familiar in the same way.
- o Look up the definition for the word know and record what you learn.
- o Mark any other repeated words or phrases that were important to you.

Interpret

Continuing to use the tool of asking questions, look back at your observations and take your answers a step further by answering these questions

- o What is the author's purpose in writing this psalm?
- o What attributes of God do you see in Psalm 139? (Record the verse where you found it)
- o Record anything else God revealed to you through His Word.

Apply/Engage with God

Because the *"Word of God is alive and active"* (Hebrews 4:12 NIV), what God reveals to you may be different than what He reveals to someone else. There are no wrong answers! God knows exactly what you need to hear and know today. Now that you have done the hard work of observing and interpreting, ask yourself the following:

- o How does your new understanding of God's Word change how you see yourself?

- o If you believed this psalm's truth, how would your attitudes and actions be different?

- o What verse stood out to you, and what do you think God is speaking to your heart through this verse and what can you do to integrate this promise of Scripture into your daily life?

Enabled through Spiritual Practice

We have just studied how meticulously and purposefully God created every part of you for His glory and how He delights in His creation of you. Do you feel the same way about yourself as God does? When you talk about your body, do you describe it as He does? When you believe and reiterate self-deprecating thoughts, you write those messages on your heart. God doesn't want you to believe those lies. It's time to write what God says about you on your heart and do it repeatedly.

Write daily reminders to yourself on your mirror with dry erase markers or with post-it notes about who God says that you are. When you see them, read them as I am statements about who you are.

I am loved.

I am chosen.

I am accepted.

I am precious.

I am redeemed.

I am victorious.

I am blameless.

I am forgiven.

I am fearfully and wonderfully made.

I am God's masterpiece.

May those words would be written on your heart and take root allowing God's lenses to remain securely fashioned over your eyes.

 Day 4
Encouraged: Ruth's Story

Being in the public eye is a difficult way to live. Although I am not a celebrity, I am the daughter of a well-known and beloved pastor in our small town where everyone knows everyone and everything that happens. People would always stop and ask me, "Aren't you Pastor Robert's daughter?" They would then continue with what a fine man he was and how they wanted me to send their best to him. Being polite, I would smile and nod, thank them, and realize most times I had no idea who they were. I could see in their eyes that they expected me to be just perfect because of my father. They really didn't see me, but only what must come from being in such a spiritual family. I had a role to live into that gave no space for mistakes.

Born first in our family, I was a high achiever. When I was young, it was easy for me to be praised for all the things I did well. I loved these comments because it made me feel good about myself, that I was loved and accepted, and that nothing would be too hard for me. It was great living the fantasy of being perfect. But middle school changed that. No longer was I on the top just by natural talent. I had to work at being excellent and I worked hard. I stayed up late at night: practicing, studying, memorizing. I was fearful of the cliff of failure I was about to fall off of for how long could I live in this cycle? People would soon be disappointed in me and no longer surround me with their love. I would be cast into the valley of normal, and I was addicted to being extraordinary. I persisted for perfection.

High school brought on the importance of my image. In my mind, so much was expected of me. The pressure of being perfect, high achieving, attractive, servant-hearted, Christ-loving, a loyal friend, top-notch athlete, and pastor's daughter became suffocating. Other kids seemed free to experiment with sex, drugs, alcohol, but I didn't because I had to stay in line with my "good Christian pastor's daughter" image; the whole town was watching me making sure I didn't make any mistakes. They would all be so disappointed in me. I worked hard at it and was successful, but it was a façade. Physically, mentally, and spiritually drained, I spent it all keeping all the important people happy.

When I went to college, I felt like I was in the abyss. No matter what I did, I failed someone. There were no accolades … no one really knew me, in fact, I didn't know who I was. My self-worth plummeted. I felt anxious, afraid, and lost during those years. No matter how hard I tried, I couldn't be perfect. There were no preconceived thoughts of me of being so good at everything. I started at square one like everyone else.

A friend shared with me that I needed to study Psalm 139 to find out who I was. I didn't believe it, I was a pastor's daughter and knew the Scriptures. There wouldn't be anything I could read in the Bible that I already didn't know. I grew up with God's Word. Grudgingly, I decided to give it a try.

The truth of God's Word impacted me greatly. The truth is that God knows everything about me: my thoughts, actions, words, longings, and body. Nothing is kept a secret from the Lord. He made me and I cannot hide from Him. His light overpowers any darkness I try to stay in. He loves me so much, more than I can imagine. My heart is His to search, test, and know all the good and evil that dwells there. He leads me from everlasting to everlasting.

I couldn't believe this. Did God really feel that way about me? Overwhelmed, I wondered why I hadn't known this before, or actually, known it for myself. I believe the Bible…I believe God. I believe that I am "intricately and skillfully formed as if embroidered with many colors in the depths of the earth." Now I had to apply that truth to my life. It is more than head knowledge; it is heart changing truth. The Creator has a vision for me. He formed it before He made me. God is delighted with me now and even more as I become what He has planned. Every day God works on me physically, spiritually, and mentally for I belong to Him.

Because of God and what I now believe, everything changed for me. I no longer believe I am created to please others but only to please One…my God. My priorities changed in what I thought was important. I no longer had to be a fake person and pretend to be excellent. I am excellent but only because of God and nothing I do. Being excellent means being what God created me to be and nothing else. My self-image greatly improved knowing that God made me and that is enough. I am His.

Engage with God

o   Ruth allowed other people's opinions of her to define her instead of God. Who do you let define you?

o   What parts of Ruth's story resonated with you?

o   How do distorted lenses contribute to your eating and body image struggles?

Enabled through Spiritual Practice

Choose one of the "I am" statements you used to remind yourself of who you are and write out the corresponding verse. Strategically place these reminders where you will see them throughout your day. Work on committing it to memory so that you can remind yourself of who you are. When we pray Scripture, we write the truth on our hearts and allow God to shape us, teach us, and heal us through His Word. Every time you read them, remember the truth of these Scriptures. May their truths replace the negative words you have been writing on your heart and write a new song upon your heart.

 ## Day 5
Entrusted and Empowered

Several years ago, a popular skin care company launched a real beauty campaign to promote positive body image among women. One video in particular highlighted how differently we see ourselves, rather than how others see us. Strangers were put in a room and asked to get to know each other while they waited. One by one, each person was asked to describe themselves to an FBI-trained sketch artist seated on the other side of the curtain. Then they were asked to describe one of the strangers they got to know in the waiting room. After all the sketches were complete, each person was able to view their self-described portrait next to that of the stranger's description. To their surprise, the description given by the stranger compared to their own was much different. The stranger's description highlighted their beauty and their own description exaggerated their perceived faults.[7] This experiment illustrates how often our perceptions of ourselves is often inaccurate and vastly different from others around us. As God transforms us, the way we see ourselves will too.

Unfortunately, holding onto that truth can be hard. We all have the opportunity to help each other remember who we are. Words are important and how we use our words affects the way we think about ourselves and the ways others feel about themselves. First Thessalonians 5:11 says, *"Encourage one another and build each other up"* (NIV). As God begins to transform your thinking, contemplate how you could share the truth of who you are with others. We all need to know we are enough, just the way God made us, yet we live in a world that preys on our insecurities. What if we complimented our friends on their character traits instead of their looks? What if we started talking about what God was doing in our lives, instead of how we feel fat? What if we started praying for our co-workers instead of engaging in gossip about them? What if we let others see the true us, flaws and all, instead of keeping up a façade? What would our world be like then? I don't know, but I'd like to find out.

Friend, stop trying to be somebody different when you already are somebody great!

Session 1

Engage with God

○ How does culture influence the way you think and feel about yourself?

○ The things that we give our time and attention to often influence us the most. What could you do differently to change your exposure to negative cultural influences?

○ What can you do to combat those influences in your own life and in the lives of others?

Enabled through Spiritual Practice

You have been encouraging yourself to change your thinking by posting Scripture throughout your daily routine. What if you could encourage someone else in the same way? Blogger Caitlyn Doyle[8] was tired of watching women pick themselves apart in front of the mirror, so she scribbled, "You Are Beautiful" on a post-it note and stuck it on the mirror of a public bathroom. This started a movement that is now called Operation Beautiful. Its mission is to post anonymous notes in public places for other people to find that communicate the message that we are all beautiful and enough just the way we are.

I challenge you to try it. Post an uplifting message on your daughter's mirror, on a friend's windshield, on a gym locker, on diet products at the grocery store, on fashion magazines at the checkout, on weight-loss books at the bookstore. Be creative! God has entrusted these truths to you, now go out and share them with someone else.

ENDNOTES

1   Thayer and Smith, "Greek Lexicon entry for Metamorphoo", *The New American Standard New Testament Greek Lexicon* (online), cited 15, May 2019, Available on the Internet: *biblestudytools.com*.
2   C. S. Lewis, *Mere Christianity* (Macmillan Publishing Company, 1943, 1980), 176.
3   "poiema," *Blue Letter Bible* (online), cited 15 May 2019, Available on the Internet: *blueletterbible.com*.
4   Nancy DeMoss Wolgenmouth, *Lies Women Believe and The Truth That Sets Them Free* (Chicago, IL: Moody Publishers, 2001), 68.
5   Holy Bible: New American Standard (La Habra, CA: The Lockman Foundation, 1960, 1995).
6   L. B. Cowman, *Streams in the Desert* (quoting George MacDonald, At the Back of the North Wind) (Grand Rapids, MI: Zondervan 1925, 1997), 160.
7   Dove Real Beauty Sketches. Available on YouTube and dove.com, 2011.
8   Caitlyn Boyle, *Operation Beautiful: Transforming the Way You See Yourself One Post-It Note at a Time* (New York, NY: Avery Publishing, 2010).

Session 2
Transformed: From Deceived to Enlightened

 **Day 1**
Enlisted to Expose the Darkness

C. S. Lewis' *Chronicles of Narnia* has long been a beloved childhood classic and an allegory of the Christian faith. In his most well-known tale, *The Lion, The Witch and The Wardrobe*,[1] Lewis introduces his readers to four siblings, two boys and two girls, who discover Narnia, an enchanted world that is ruled by the evil White Witch who has decreed an eternal winter. First the youngest girl, Lucy, discovers a portal to Narnia in a large wardrobe. The other siblings don't believe her. Then Edmund, the younger of the two boys and the biggest scoffer of Lucy, discovers Narnia himself and meets the White Witch. She has heard of the four siblings and knows they are a threat to fulfill the prophecy to end her reign. She woos Edmund by his stomach, offering him a hot elixir and Turkish delight. The White Witch promises Edmund that if he brings his siblings to her castle that she'll make him a prince and he can eat all the Turkish delight he wants, when in actuality she planned to kill them all to secure her throne.

Isn't this a picture of us too? Time and again, the enemy lures us in with tantalizing and tempting offers to fulfill our deep-seated fleshy desires only to be rewarded with deception and betrayal. Adam and Eve ate from the forbidden tree thinking they would be more like God, but instead sin entered the world (Genesis 3). Jacob tricked Esau to give him his birthright for a bowl of stew (Genesis 25). For 30 pieces of silver Judas betrayed Jesus, setting in motion His death (Matthew 26). Isn't it just how it works with us? Satan is not creative and uses the same strategies against us that he used back in the garden. He is a crafty enemy who slowly and methodically steers us off-course with lies being one of his most effective tactics. It is easy to become ensnared by lies, especially when they seem so enticing. This week, we will work on creating our own defensive and offensive strategies to fight against Satan and his schemes.

Engage with God

o   How have you fallen prey to the enemy's lies and schemes?

o   How can the truths you learned about yourself in session 1 help you safeguard yourself from becoming ensnared by the enemy?

Enabled through Spiritual Practice

We just studied who God says we are in the last session. Are you telling yourself the truth about who you are, or are you entertaining lies? As followers of God, we are called to be truth speakers and that includes being a truth speaker to ourselves. Our thoughts greatly influence who we think we are, which in turn influences how we treat ourselves. I would guess you would never tell your best friend her thighs were too fat, she'll never be good enough, or that she's a complete failure. Those sound like words for your worst enemy, yet I would guess you say the same kinds of things to yourself every day. Are you treating yourself like your best friend or like your worst enemy? If you fall closer on the spectrum to worst enemy, I would guess there are some lies that need weeding out. In order to fight against lies you are believing and know what we're up against, you first need to identify them.

Start by making a T chart. At the top of the left-hand column, write "Lies I believe about myself." At the top of the right-hand column, write "Who God says I am." Ask God to reveal any lies you are believing about yourself. As you identify them, list them in the left-hand column. Once you have your list, find a Scripture that unmasks the lie and states the truth about who you are and list them in the right-hand column. Then each time that lie appears in your thought life, replace it with the truth you uncovered from God's Word. Record any new insights, changes in thoughts, or attitudes as a result of this practice.

Day 2
Entangled by Sin

If we are going to try and fight against the enemy's schemes, then we need to understand what we are up against. In this section, we will be utilizing Nancy DeMoss Wolgemuth's outline of Eve's deception from her book *Lies Young Women Believe and the Truth that Sets Them Free*.[2] Here are the different stages we will be walking through together:

1. Eve LISTENED to the lie by entertaining his suggestion
2. Eve DWELLED on the lie by considering what he said
3. Eve BELIEVED the lie instead of God's Truth
4. Eve ACTED on the lie by eating the fruit.

Let's look at this progression a little more closely. Eve's first mistake was that she stayed around long enough to hear what the serpent had to say. Don't we do the same thing when we expose ourselves to things that we know probably aren't God's best for us. Imagine this scenario: you are online checking email and an advertisement pops up on the side bar that says, "Tips and tricks to have the beach body you've always dreamed about." You find yourself thinking this is probably just a scam, but soon you're entertaining the idea, wondering if it would really work. You now have the choice before you of clicking on it or not. What are you going to do?

God gives us an example of what we should do in Genesis 39:12 when Potiphar's wife approaches Joseph. It says, *"She caught him by his cloak and said, 'Come to bed with me!' But he left his cloak in her hand and ran out of the house."* That is what you need to do when you are tempted to hang around and listen to the lie—drop your coat and run! Prayerfully ask God what things may lead you into temptation and then do your best to stay away from it at all costs.

However, we often choose not to run and instead click on the link, exposing ourselves to more ammo in favor of the lie. Just like Eve, we begin to dwell on the tempting prospect in front of us. Reading through the tips and tricks causes you to consider the possibility that this formula could actually work for me. Your thoughts jump off the starting block. You begin pondering at break neck speed new levels of happiness, satisfaction, acceptance, and approval as a result. Just like Eve you begin to question God and His ways, wondering if God is withholding something from you. Eve felt entitled to the knowledge that came from the forbidden tree and failed to see that God had placed limits on her to protect her from things she knew nothing about, but her Sovereign Lord did.

Because Eve kept thinking about what the serpent had said, she began to believe that he was right. You find yourself in the same situation. Your thoughts plunge you forward into a web of lies, and you believe that your happiness and livelihood depends on doing something to change your current disparaging state. Feelings of worthlessness, hopelessness, and shame flood your mind and cloud your perception of reality.

The result of Eve's contemplative process was action. Eve ate the apple. Lies unchecked by truth are a recipe for destruction because they lead to action. In our scenario, engaging in these "tips and tricks" which don't satisfy lead you to seek other solutions. This can quickly turn into self-harming, consuming behaviors that preoccupy all your time and energy but leave you no more satisfied than when you started. You wake up one day realizing you've been betrayed. You never achieved the happiness, approval, and fulfillment your dream promised you. Rather, you are enslaved. You never intended to end up here, but Satan slowly, subtly, deceivingly led you to your demise all with a seemingly harmless click of a button.

Maybe you think my example is far-fetched. You might be right, but I believed the lies. Lies of needing to prove I was worthwhile, fearing others wouldn't love me if I failed, convincing myself everything wrong was my fault. Believing these lies led me into the destructive pattern of an eating disorder. I became trapped by things I thought would make me happy and free but instead I felt hopeless, depressed, and alone. It wasn't until God exposed the lies I had believed and replaced them with His Truth that I found freedom, hope, and contentment.

Engage with God

o   What lies are you believing?

o   How many of those lies are keeping you trapped in a pattern of destructive behavior? Which ones and why?

o   How can you stop yourself from listening, dwelling, and believing in those lies so they don't lead to action?

Enabled through Spiritual Practice

The practice of speaking truth to yourself about who you are will take some time to implement. Dr. Caroline Leaf in her book *Switch on Your Brain*[3] talks about the science behind your thought life and how you can retrain your brain to think differently. She explains that it takes 21 days to replace toxic thoughts with healthy ones. With that in mind, look back at your T chart and pick one lie that you would like to focus on replacing. Using the corresponding verse you found to counteract the lie, create an "I am" statement using that truth. For example if your lie was "I am a mistake," you would tell yourself, "I am fearfully and wonderfully made," based on Psalm 139:14. Try starting each day for the next three weeks with that I am statement and record any changes to your thought life.

Day 3
Enlightened through Scripture Study

Pray

Lord, thank You that You are the God of Truth. Give me eyes to see and ears to hear Your truth instead of lies. I confess I have been believing lies. Shine your light into the dark places of my heart and expose any lies that I am believing and replace them with truth. In Jesus' name I pray, amen.

Observe

Passage: Genesis 3:1-6 (NIV)

Identifying contrasts helps to show us how two things are different.

o   Mark in the passage the four areas of Eve's listening, dwelling, believing, and acting on the lie. Then, contrast what God actually said and what the serpent quoted God as saying by reading Genesis 2:15-17.

o   In verse 1, the serpent creates doubt by saying, *"Did God really say..."* (NIV). (Underline that phrase every time it appears). Is there any mention of God in that verse? What does that reveal to you?

Interpret

Context is key to understanding the meaning of selected verses. By cross-referencing other areas of Scripture, we can confirm our interpretation since Scripture never contradicts itself. You already cross-referenced Genesis 2 above, now try reading Matthew 5:43-44 in NASB.

o   Record the first phrase of each verse. In order to understand who is speaking, you will need to read a bit more in that chapter to understand the context.

o   Note that one section of the verse is in all caps. What does that tell you?

o   Did you notice that the all caps section is quoting one of the Ten Commandments, but the second part of that verse is not? This indicates that the Pharisees were adding something to the law that wasn't from the Lord. Can you see the subtle shift and how it changes the meaning? How does this relate to the passage in Genesis?

Apply/Engage with God

o   Are there any areas of your life from which God has been slowly and subtly become nonexistent, and what can you do to refocus those areas to allow God to reign in them again?

o   Do you ever feel restricted by God's boundaries or feel like God is withholding things from you? If so, how do you respond to those feelings?

o   What did God reveal to you through the passage? Are there any changes you need to make as a result?

Enabled through Spiritual Practice

Another way to prevent lies from impeding our thought life is to decrease our exposure to them by means of fasting. Fasting may seem like a spiritual excuse to lose weight, but that is far from the true intent of the discipline. Fasting gives you the opportunity to sacrifice an appetite in order to become more in tune with God and feast on Him. We have lots of different appetites that stretch far beyond food, and we often try and meet them with things that are not from God. Unmet longings act as a breeding ground for lies to develop and fuel destructive patterns. Therefore, consider asking the Lord to help you identify and fast from something that is feeding the lies, something not food related. Maybe it's self-deprecating comments, maybe it's social media, maybe it's magazines, maybe it's romance novels? Take some time to pray today and ask God what He might be prompting you to fast. More on how to go about fasting tomorrow.

 **Day 4**
Encouraged: My Story

You messed up again. I knew you couldn't do it right. You're just not good enough. This is all your fault. You're such a failure. I can't believe you're even struggling with this. You're worthless. No one will ever love you…

These are the lies I constantly heard. They colored my view of me, my circumstance, and just about everything in my life. Their volume surged at those moments of doubt and darkness. I entertained the lies instead of discarding them and started to believe them. These lies sapped my attention, my thoughts, and my energies. I still engaged with the truth but became lost in a sea of lies. Soon the lies consumed all my thinking and, sadly, they seemed more real to me than truth.

Believing the lies caused me to stray off-course and the less I liked myself. The tapes in my mind played repeatedly, and I became desperate to lessen their frequency and intensity. I became convinced that if I could just recreate how I used to be when I felt loved and accepted, then that would fix things. But how?

Shortly thereafter, I started receiving positive comments from others about how I looked. "You look great! Did you lose weight?" "Are you working out?" I was surprised because losing weight was not on my radar. My mind was preoccupied with listening to these tapes and little else. But their comments made me feel good. Suddenly the thought occurred to me, "Oh no, what if I gain weight? Then they'll be disappointed in me too. I had better not gain any weight." I thought this would be the avenue to fix my problems and make me acceptable again.

Not gaining weight was my new goal, which translated into me becoming preoccupied with how much I was eating. I feared that I was going to eat too much and gain weight. This thought pattern resulted in me eating less and less. I also decided to "get healthy" and created a strict daily exercise regime. I set out to prove those lies wrong and my eating disorder was born. The eating disorder tempted me with empty promises of beauty, acceptance, worthiness, and success. None of those things occurred. Instead, it betrayed me and left me broken, consumed, and with a new master taking God's place on the throne of my heart.

I did lose weight. People did notice. I got a lot of positive comments at first, and that felt good. However, my weight continued to steadily decrease to the tune of 50 lbs. in less than a year. I became emaciated. The positive comments stopped. The eating disorder was no longer helping me reach my goal, but I was too entrenched to stop it. A few people spoke up and expressed concern, but it all just sounded like another disappointment.

Now the tapes were blaring non-stop with more ammo than ever before. I knew I needed help, but I was too proud to admit I had a problem and was in denial of how big a problem it had become. Instead, I tried to pull away from people, avoid eating socially, and hide behind a façade of happiness. I convinced myself that no one knew. Another lie.

Physical complications began from not eating enough. I couldn't sit comfortably because pain would shoot down my legs, my hands and feet were discolored because my circulation was so poor, and I was cold all the time. My hair became dull and started to fall out. While this was unnerving, I also had a few scares that awakened me to realize that I was on a path of death not life. As you can imagine, this not only affected me negatively but those around me as well.

Motivated to get help and get better, I asked experts to just give me a plan, so I could get better. I wanted three simple steps to get back on track, but there was no such formula. I soon discovered that I had allowed the eating disorder to grow so large that it wasn't going to give up mastery over me quickly or easily.

For the next seven years, I fought back. Battles were won, and battles were lost, but I kept fighting. Then one day, my treatment team told me how great I was doing and that I was probably as good as I'd ever get. What?!! Seriously? But it's not gone! This kind of fear is natural when you have depended on a team of people to help you. These people were the experts, and they knew it was time for me to take control of managing my disorder.

"Eating disorders don't ever go away; they just have to be managed," they said. I had been working this hard for seven years and for what? This was devastating to me. So, I quit. I quit trying to get better. I quit trying to please everyone. I quit fighting back. This led to a relapse that was darker, deeper, and disturbing. I was rapidly losing weight again. My treatment team had never seen me unmotivated and didn't know what to do with me. Hopelessness set in, and it became harder to see what purpose I had in life.

My thoughts grew dark, and I didn't feel like myself. I reached out to a trusted friend. I shared how I felt, how I didn't feel like myself, and how I was scared. She started praying for me, and God began to move in a mighty way. Our prayer time together started a chain of events, where God uncovered the lies I believed and showed me how they were keeping me stuck. It was like God turned on the light in a dark room and exposed all that was hiding inside. As truth began to permeate the lies, the tapes grew softer, more infrequent, and eventually stopped all together. My urges to engage in eating disorder behaviors dissipated. God had reclaimed the throne of my heart and His truth has set me free.

Engage with God

o   Lies led me astray until I became entrenched in eating disorder behaviors and patterns. How do lies lead you astray?

o   How do those lies contribute specifically to your eating and body image struggles?

o   What parts of my story resonated with you?

Enabled through Spiritual Practice

Once you have identified what God is asking you to fast from, plan some tangible steps you can take to replace those old habits and feast on the things of God instead. For example:

o   Only check email three times a day or set aside one day a week to respond to emails. Use the time you would have used to deal with email to pray.
o   Decide not to buy, look at, or read magazines. Instead, spend that time reading Scripture. Install a Bible app and begin a daily reading plan.
o   Put a sticker over the Facebook app on your phone so you can't access it or use a screen time app to make apps go to sleep after a set period of time.

Once the parameters are in place, determine how long you will stay on the fast and make accommodations to stick to the plan. When we fast from things that require a lot of our time, energy, and resources, we can begin to feast on the things of God. Not only is it important to open our hearts to God, but we need to have a teachable spirit. We can acquire lots of knowledge, but that does not equate to change unless we have teachable spirits. Having a teachable spirit means that you hear truth and are able to apply it to your life by making the necessary changes. God calls us to be lifelong learners, continually growing, adapting, and maturing in our walk with Him.

Day 5
Entrusted and Empowered

This week you uncovered the pattern of how listening, dwelling, and believing lies leads to destructive actions, just as Satan intended. As the enemy bombards our minds with lies, he would like us to believe that we are powerless to change anything, dragging our "sins behind us with ropes made of lies" (Isaiah 5:18 NLT). In her book *The Armor of God*, Priscilla Shirer describes the enemy's strategy this way,

> *"Your enemy wants to distract you. So he can blindside you. And listen to me—he is not indiscriminately shooting these arrows of his. He is tailored in his strategy. He studies your tendencies and habits, your deepest fears and weaknesses, and has aimed at those areas in particular. He knows he can't destroy you. You're eternally secure in Jesus. But he fully intends to sidetrack your attention by setting any number of internal fires ablaze in your life—like insecurity, intimidation, anxiety, worry or busyness. He wants you to be unfocused while he sneaks up from behind."[4]*

This eye-opening quote by Priscilla awakens us to the reality that our enemy is real and out to destroy us. The Apostle Peter gives us the same warning when he says, *"Be alert and of sober mind. Your enemy the devil prowls around like a roaring lion looking for someone to devour. Resist him by standing firm in the faith"* (1 Peter 5:8-9a NIV).

The battle is raging in the spiritual realm, but God does not send us into battle ill-equipped and powerless, although Satan wants us to believe the lie that He does. However, we as Christians are not powerless. Jesus overcame death and sin and that same power is in us too. First John 4:4 says, *"But you belong to God, my dear children. You have already won a victory over those people, because the Spirit who lives in you is greater than the spirit who lives in the world"* (NLT).

God gave us both offensive and defensive weapons of warfare cataloged in Ephesians 6 to empower and equip us for battle. Our defensive weapons are the helmet of salvation, the breastplate of righteousness, the belt of truth, gospel shoes, and the shield of faith. We are encouraged to *"put on the full armor of God, so that [we] can take [our] stand against the devil's schemes"* (Ephesians 6:11 NIV). I don't know about you, but I wouldn't want to show up for battle with nothing to protect myself. Each morning as you're getting dressed, try "praying your armor on" so you are ready for whatever battle may come that day.

Now that you have your protective armor on, what do you do if you're attacked? Pull out your offensive weapon, the sword of the Spirit also known as the Word of God. You already know you've got Jesus' victory power in you. All we have to do to tap into that power is speak the name of Jesus or a verse(s) from God's Word. The enemy cannot read our thoughts, so we must speak it out loud. This may seem awkward at first. But the enemy must flee when the name of Jesus or God's Word is spoken. Next time the enemy tries to attack, you'll be ready. So put on your armor and fight, you courageous daughter of the King!

Engage with God

o   What will your battle strategy look like when you feel attacked by lies from the enemy?

o   What barriers do you fear will keep you from implementing your new battle strategy, and what can you do to prevent them?

Enabled through Spiritual Practice

Put the offensive weapon into practice by speaking Scripture out loud. Do it often. Saturate your mind with truth. For "they shall know the truth and the truth will set them free" (John 8:32 NIV). Here are a few concrete ideas I've collected from women in my classes to add to your arsenal.

o   Select the verse that resonates with you most and write it on a notecard. Keep the notecard readily accessible. Next time you catch yourself entertaining that lie, take out your card and read it out loud. One woman decided to remind herself often by making the verse as the wallpaper on her phone.

o   Why limit yourself to one notecard? Buy a spiral bound 3x5 card booklet (or create your own). Write out Scripture verses to counteract lies you believe. Carry the notecards with you so you can read through the Scripture verses when you feel attacked. Another woman created a collection of hundreds of verses and read them while she ate a meal. Sometimes it was the only way she could get through it without engaging in a self-harming behavior.

o   If you learn best by hearing, make an audio recording of the verses that you can play back to flood your mind with Scripture. Another woman would put on headphones and play an audio version of the Bible to drown out her unwanted thoughts. Otherwise, they were too loud for her to hear anything else.

o   After you try some of these exercises, write about it in your journal. Describe your experience. How did it make you feel? Was there a difference before and after?

ENDNOTES

1   C. S. Lewis, *The Chronicles of Narnia: The Lion, The Witch and The Wardrobe* (New York, NY: HarperTrophy, 1994).
2   Nancy DeMoss Wolgenmouth and Dannah Gresh, *Lies Young Women Believe and The Truth That Sets Them Free* (Chicago, IL: Moody Publishers, 2009), Chapter 2, 27-33.
3   Dr. Caroline Leaf, *Switch On Your Brain* (Grand Rapids, MI: Baker Books, 2015).
4   Priscilla Shirer, *The Armor of God* (Nashville, TN: LifeWay Press, 2015), 130.

Session 3
Transformed: From Fearful to Fearless

 **Day 1**
Enlisted to Expose the Darkness

Are you afraid of sharks? I am. Ever since I was a little girl, I was afraid to swim in the ocean fearing that a shark would come out of nowhere and turn me into his lunch. I had no problem swimming in a swimming pool or lake, but put me in the ocean and I'd freak out. I'd like to say I grew out of it, but just this month my family went on a cruise and my fear of sharks was exposed again. As we talked about what activities to do, my husband suggested taking a boat to a nearby reef to go snorkeling. I was hesitant to say yes because I was thinking about the potential risks I would be taking. My husband noticed my hesitation and asked me what was wrong. I tried to come up with a list of reasons why it didn't seem like a good idea. After listing several convincing arguments, I mentioned sharks at the end. My husband said, "Now let me get this straight. Your biggest fear of this experience is not the rough sea waters, capsizing, drowning, jellyfish stings, or equipment malfunction. It's sharks?" I looked at him and replied sheepishly, "Yes." My husband cited the odds of me getting attacked by a shark as 1 in 11.5 million. Despite the odds, I was still afraid. Clearly, my fear was not based in reality, but that did not make it any less palpable or easier to overcome.

While it's important to have a healthy fear of the creatures of the sea when you are in their environment, my irrational and unhealthy fear of being eaten by a shark kept me from experiencing and enjoying a wonderful opportunity. In the same way, a healthy fear of the Lord and of danger keeps us safe and walking on a path of obedience, whereas, an unhealthy fear can keep us from doing or experiencing all that God has for us. Fear itself isn't the problem; rather, it's our response to it that can get us into trouble. How often do we let fear keep us from having a difficult conversation, sharing about Jesus with our neighbor, or taking a step of faith? How can you live the life God has called you to if you are paralyzed by anxiety and fear?

Engage with God

Stormie Omartian describes fear as **F**alse **E**vidence **A**ppearing **R**eal.[1] Fear can be like a funhouse mirror, distorting an image and making it appear vastly different than reality.

o   Make a list of the things you are afraid of. As you look at your list, ask God to help you discern which fears fall into that category and circle them. Are those fears rationally or irrationally based? Explain.

o   What do you fear will happen if you do those things, and how does that fear keep you from doing what God is asking you to do?

Enabled through Spiritual Practice

Whether rational or irrational, fear can manifest physiologically causing panic attacks, difficulty breathing or feeling paralyzed to move. Psalm 116:11 says, *"In my anxiety, I called out to you"* (NLT). When you find yourself struggling with fear and anxiety, try calling out to God through "breath prayer." This is a means of meditating on a specific truth of Scripture by incorporating calming breathing techniques to help if you are experiencing a physiological response. As you inhale, silently pray the first part of the phrase, and as you exhale, pray the second part. Here are a few suggestions. Feel free to use one of the verses listed below or use Scripture to create your own. Each time you find yourself grappling with fear, spend a few moments reorienting your thinking.

Here are a few Scriptures for you to try:

> Isaiah 30:15 (inhale) quietness and trust—(exhale) shall be my strength
> Psalm 84:12 (inhale) God blesses—(exhale) those who trust
> Psalm 20:17 (inhale) I trust—(exhale) in the Lord's name
> Psalm 118:6 (inhale) The LORD is for me—(exhale) I will have no fear

 Day 2
Entangled by Sin

Sometimes our emotions overwhelm us, and we are either quick to label them good or bad or tell ourselves how we should or shouldn't feel. The reality is that emotions are neither good nor bad, they just are. So fear, like all emotions, gives us helpful information. For example, fear helps us make decisions that keep us out of danger. We teach our children not to touch a hot stove, not to take candy from strangers, and to look both ways before crossing the street. Also, when we hold reverent fear of God in regard to His power, His might, and His sovereignty, it fuels our desire to live in accordance with God's way.

Emotions often color our experiences influencing our thoughts and feelings. While God gave us emotions, our decisions must rely on God's promises, not our ever changing emotions. Fear may help keep us out of danger, but when we let it entangle our thought life, we can become enslaved to it. Fear then begins to grip us, debilitate us, control us, paralyze us, consume us, and we find ourselves captive to it. We are so afraid of what might happen in the future that it keeps us from living abundant lives as God intended. When we let fear take over, it paralyzes us. When we let God take over, it empowers us.

Fear became an influential component, a driving force, a fixture of my eating disorder. Most, if not all, of my decisions were made from a root of fear. I feared eating the "wrong" things, eating too much, eating too often, gaining weight, eating socially, trying new things, what others thought of me, disapproval from others, rejection, abandonment, failure, and the list went on. It was as though my fears had imprisoned me. While I held the keys to unlock the door, I was terrified to do it. You see, I had grown accustomed to my self-made prison walls. Though they kept me captive, at least I knew what to expect from them. The unknowns I would face as a result of leaving my figurative prison seemed more frightening than staying, so fear kept me enchained.

This kind of fear is not from the Lord: *"God has not given us a spirit of fear, but of power and of love and of a sound mind"* (2 Timothy 1:7 NKJV).[2] The Bible has a lot to say about fear; in fact the word is used roughly 350 times (varies with different translations) throughout Scripture, often illustrating how people responded to their fears. In these Scriptural examples, we see the fruit of obedience contrasted with the devastation of fear-based decision-making. Undoubtedly, fear has been and continues to be a stumbling block for humanity. Billy Graham said it well:

> *"Historians will probably call our era 'the age of anxiety.' Anxiety is the natural result when our hopes are centered in anything short of God and His will for us."*

If we live this way, we run the risk of living fear-filled lives, hoping in the things of this world and buying into its lies. Instead, we must fix our eyes on Jesus (Hebrews 12:2 NIV) and allow God to transform our fear into trust. We can accomplish this by training ourselves to turn to God for help and by trusting in Him for rescue (Psalm 56:3 NIV). Psalm 118:5 says, *"In my distress I prayed to the LORD and the LORD answered me"* (NLT). This call and response paradigm appears over 40 times in the Psalms alone and demonstrates for us how we are to respond when we find ourselves in distress. This model shifts our focus, our trust, and our hope back onto God as we wait for the answer that He promises to give.

I understand that changing ingrained patterns is difficult and takes more time than we'd like to give. However, what if we adopted a new radical way of thinking? What if we decided that instead of living imprisoned by fear, we decided to live fearlessly? Living fearlessly means that we will not let fear or anything else entangle us but instead stand firm on God's promises in faith and in trust. What if we chose to believe that God is who He says He is and that He will do what He says He is going to do? What if we determined to not be intimidated or discouraged by difficulty, danger, or disappointment? What if we resolved to step out of our respective prison cells and never return because we can trust that what God has for us is immeasurably more than we could ask for or imagine (Ephesians 3:20)?

Beloved, I challenge you to place all your fears in a box, not to hide them but as an offering to God. Entrust your fears to Him and leave them in the capable hands of Jesus at the place at the foot of the cross. Know you can visit your box of fears anytime you want to in prayer, but let Him hold on to them, so they don't hold on to you.

> *"So, do not fear, for I am with you; do not be dismayed, for I am your God. I will strengthen you and help you; I will uphold you with my righteous right hand"* (Isaiah 41:10 NIV).

Engage with God

o   In what ways do you feel imprisoned by fear?

o   How might lies you're believing be contributing to the fears you have?

o   What can you do differently in order to live fearlessly instead of fearfully?

Enabled through Spiritual Practice

It is important to pay attention to the different signals our bodies send to us. We already discussed how our fears can manifest in our bodies physiologically. Today we will hone in on dissecting these physiological cues by identifying them, analyzing them without judging, learning from them, and then turning them over to God.

Identify: Find a peaceful place and quiet yourself before the Lord. Then, think of your biggest fear. As your mind begins to process your fear, notice how your body feels. Describe it.

o   Maybe you feel tense. Describe where you feel that in your body.
o   Maybe you notice a change in appetite. Describe if it increases or decreases.
o   Maybe you notice a change in your thinking. Is your mind racing or shutting down to sleep?
o   Take note of any other emotions you are feeling, in addition to being afraid.

Analyze: Look back over your responses without jumping to judgment. You are merely analyzing data or facts.

o   Are there any patterns?
o   Do different situations evoke a similar response or a different response?

Learn: After you've looked over your analysis, ask God what He would want you to know about your fear and how you respond to it. Record what you learn.

Turn over: Using breath prayer, practice turning that fear over to God and entrusting Him with it.

Day 3
Enlightened through Scripture Study

Pray

Lord, I am so afraid. I confess the ways fear keeps me from acting in obedience to You. Thank You that You are not a God of fear but one of power, love, and a sound mind (2 Timothy 1:7). I pray that You would remove all fear from my heart and replace it with a renewed trust in You. Help me to turn to You the second I feel afraid and may You "quiet my heart with your love" (Zephaniah 3:17 NIV). In Jesus' name I pray, amen.

Observe

Passage: Psalm 37 (NIV)

When we observe verbs in the imperative form (also known as commands), they often give us instructions or directives about how we should live our lives. As you read Psalm 37, mark all the phrases in the imperative tense or in command form. For example: verse 1 says, "Do not worry" and verse 3 says, "Trust in the LORD and do good."

- o Lists help highlight important concepts. Make a list of all of the commands/imperatives in the passage.
- o Are the phrases in the imperative tense written for the godly or the wicked? Is their purpose to encourage, instruct, direct, discipline, or warn?

Note that commands here are given in the present tense, describing things God is encouraging, exhorting, or directing us to do. The future tense often follows the command, describing what God will do as a result.

- o Reread the passage and mark the word "will."
- o Make a list recording what will happen as a result of obeying God's commands.

Interpret

The future tense is often used in conjunction with prophecy. *Prophecy* means predicting what will happen in the future. Because God stands outside of time, He can make predictions about what will happen. Because He is Sovereign and in control, He will fulfill His promises.

- o Make two columns. In one column list the inheritance of the godly or those who trust in the Lord. In the other column list the inheritance of the wicked. Be sure to indicate the verse where you found it next to each phrase you write down.
- o Your T chart helped you note the inheritance of the godly in contrast to the inheritance of the wicked. Contrasts can be readily spotted by looking for the word "but." How does this contrast help you understand how God views the godly and the wicked?

Apply/Engage with God

As you review your work, let it soak in how God rewards those who trust in Him.

- o Review the commands given in the passage. Ask God if any of the commands apply to you. Record what you learn.

- o Are there any changes you need to make in order to find yourself among those counted as godly, and how does this knowledge help you trust God in a new way?

o   What verse stood out most to you? What do you feel God is saying to you through it?

Note: *Let me clarify who the wicked are in God's eyes. The wicked are those described as stiff-necked, stubborn, and hard hearted, as those who have been long living in habitual sin with no regard for God's ways; refusing to turn back to God even when warned. Their sin does not change how God feels about them, meaning He still loves them, but their habitual sin does have consequences in God's kingdom as referenced here. It does not refer to those who make a concerted effort to pursue godliness yet still get tripped up by sin and are repentant of it.*

Enabled through Spiritual Practice

As you continue to use breath prayer to help you ease your fears, take the verse from Psalm 37 that stood out to you and use it for your breath prayer today. I am practicing with verse 5.

Psalm 37:5 (inhale) Trust in the Lord—(exhale) He will do this.

Visualize how you will use breath prayer throughout your day to help you ease your fears. Will you do it out loud? Will you do it in your head? Will you close your eyes? Will you do it at a stoplight? Will you stop in the middle of the grocery store? Will you excuse yourself to the bathroom? Make a plan so that you are ready to implement it when you feel your fears rising.

When God says He will do this, He means He *will do this*. Stand on the promises God has made. He can never contradict Himself because that goes against His character. When you pray, pray with confidence that God will fulfill His promises. God knows you are afraid. Call upon Him to help you, and He will answer you.

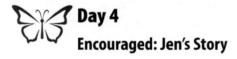 **Day 4**
Encouraged: Jen's Story

Why was this happening to me? At 22, the severe pain of fibromyalgia struck me. Married for just over a year, my husband and I were shocked at the sudden change in our lives together. Daily, I have constant debilitating pain that left our lives in shambles.

My faith was weak at that time. I believed that I deserved to live this way and resorted to what I had always done to handle problems. Performance.

Performance told me my worth. This I learned from a very early age. If I did something well, I was praised, which made me feel loved. If I did something wrong or not good enough, I felt shame, which made me feel unloved. The fear of feeling shame and unloved is what fueled my fire to always do. I never felt free or safe to just be. So, when I began to feel the shame of being cursed with a chronic illness, I made the decision to do my best to deal with it.

I followed the orders of doctors times ten. In addition to the arsenal of prescription drugs and physical therapy, I would exercise two to three times a day to try to feel better. I also ate very little because of the onset of G/I issues that fibromyalgia patients often experience. This resulted in my loss of 50 pounds in less than three months. When people saw me, they would gush at how "good" and "healthy" I looked and assumed I was feeling better. I let them and learned very quickly that I could fool everyone. By looking good on the outside, they would never question what was really happening on the inside.

My appearance became my obsession. This distracted people so they wouldn't ask about my illness. I covered up my pain with designer labels and a fit, trim body, numbed my mind with prescription drugs, and escaped my agony every night via hefty sleeping pills. I would not be labeled, pitied, or judged, so I hid myself and acted as if life was great for me. This was my lot in life. I justified my behavior by thinking a positive attitude would be my mask, knowing no one would understand what I was going through anyway.

Those were dark times. I spiraled in my superficial life, lived with a shattered heart. Destruction was before me. My marriage was broken even as my husband continually prayed for my life. Then God did something quite unexpected. I became pregnant.

I went on my knees in fear. I begged the Lord for help. I knew I couldn't continue on the destructive path I was on, because my life wasn't just about me anymore. I needed God to protect our child from the harm I had been doing to my body and help me detox from the drugs. I heard the Lord tell my heart, "It hasn't been about you this whole time. I've been with you all along." I knew that everything was going to be okay. God delivered to us our beautiful daughter, Emalynn Elizabeth, who was born eight months later, healthy, strong, and a wonderful gift from the Lord.

Over the next four and a half years, two more miracles arrived as our sons Maxwell and Jackson were born. Although these should have been happy times, I still hid behind my role as a wife and mother as my identity in fear of anyone seeing the real me. I never spoke of my illness or the constant dependence I had on the Lord to survive, especially without narcotics for relief. It broke my heart that I lived in constant fear of being judged or misunderstood by even those closest to me. I continued to hide.

When our youngest child was almost a year old, I realized that I was living life as a liar. That was wrong and I had to change. I needed to come clean and be honest. Though I was terrified, I knew it was time. I told my story to thousands of people at Christmas and experienced relief through finally being who I am rather than what I was doing to achieve acceptance.

My health has not improved over the years; in fact, it has declined to where I have needed several surgeries including a hysterectomy and an electric spinal stimulator. The emotional pain is often harder than physical pain. Many times I have given into fear and let my hope in the Lord fade. The enemy wants me there so my faith will waver and my fear will grow. He wants the promises and faithfulness of God to be forgotten. The enemy desires me to hide behind my appearance. I continually battle to believe truth rather than lies about who I am in Christ. I grip the shield of faith to guard my heart against fear. It is essential.

Engage with God

Fear kept Jen from experiencing her life fully and caused her to turn to other things to ease her fears.

- o   What parts of Jen's story resonated with you?

- o   How does fear contribute to your eating and body image struggles?

- o   Are there any ways fear is keeping you from taking the steps needed in order to be a healthier person emotionally, physically and spiritually?

Enabled through Spiritual Practice

One year, a friend of mine had the boldness—or better yet, the audacity—to give up her depression for Lent. I was blown away by the concept. She implemented a radical idea by taking small tangible steps. Every time her fears began to overwhelm her and feelings of despair would arise, she would do things like breath prayer to turn her thoughts over to God. As she trusted God over and over again with her feelings, the weight of their burden decreased. In essence God was transforming her depression, one prayer at a time.

In what situations did you find yourself feeling fearful and how has breath prayer helped you to remember to turn to God? Think of someone in your life who struggles with fear and could benefit from learning breath prayer. Share with them how it has helped you to turn to God when you're afraid, and teach them how to use it when fear strikes them.

 Day 5
Entrusted and Empowered

It's one thing to say you trust God. It's another thing to trust God when you are afraid. Even though God had rescued me from my eating disorder and shown me that He was trustworthy, I still found myself afraid. Could I trust Him to bring me through yet another deep valley of suffering? *"As for me, I look to the LORD for His help. I wait CONFIDENTLY for God to save me, and my God will certainly hear me"* (Micah 7:7 NLT). Wait confidently, with certainty? When I'm afraid, confidence and certainty are the exact opposite of how I feel. I realized it was because I kept thinking the outcome rested on my shoulders when in actuality it rested on God's. God was asking me to give my fears over to Him and trust Him, but I didn't know what that looked like.

As I studied the Psalms, I was surprised by how often the psalmist prays in commands. Meaning when he prays, he doesn't sheepishly skirt around his request. No, he pleads with God saying things like, "Save Me," "Heal Me," "Rescue Me," "Help Me," and "Vindicate Me." I thought, how could David be so bold as to pray this way? It's because David's confidence rested in God, not in himself. David knew that the God he was crying out to was the same God who created the world and all that is in it. The same God who flooded the earth, parted the Red Sea, turned the Nile into blood, and performed countless other wonders and miracles. The same God who made up a plan to save all of humanity through His Son Jesus Christ. Even though David had a lot to fear, he prayed big because he lived in *"confident dependence"* (Hosea 12:6 NLT) on our amazing God.

We pray to the same amazing God David did. Don't let fear hinder your prayer life by limiting our limitless God. The next time you're facing difficult circumstances, pray like you remember how great God is and that He is on your side.

> *"But blessed is the one who trusts in the LORD, whose confidence is in Him. They will be like a tree planted by the water that sends out its roots by the stream. It does not fear when heat comes; its leaves are always green. It has no worries in a year of drought and never fails to bear fruit"* (Jeremiah 17:7-8 NIV).

Engage with God

o   What would it take for you to be confident in the face of fear. knowing that God is on your side?

o   How can you help encourage someone in your life by sharing these truths with them in the midst of their trial?

Enabled through Spiritual Practice

Here is an activity to try with your friends, your family, or your group to get them thinking about trusting in the Lord. Set up a small obstacle course in your room. Select a volunteer who is willing to allow themselves to be blindfolded while the leader verbally guides them through the course. Add in some other distractions to make it harder for the volunteer to hear the leader's voice. This could be anything from people talking and moving around to a variety of different background noises.

Discuss what you observed and how it parallels our walk of faith with God. Remark what helped the volunteer succeed and what caused her problems. I encourage you to read 1 Kings 19 as a group which chronicles Elijah's story of learning how to listen and discern God's voice.

This exercise doesn't work unless the person blindfolded can trust the person who is guiding them, does it? The same is true in our relationship with God. It's nearly impossible to receive spiritual direction from the Lord if we don't believe that He is trustworthy, and the result is fear.

Discussion Questions

o   What can you do to let go of fear and put your trust in God?

o   What obstacles stand in your way of believing God is trustworthy?

o   What action steps can you take to remove the obstacles?

ENDNOTES

1   Stormie Omartian, *The Power of a Praying Parent* (Eugene, OR: Harvest House Publishers, Inc.), 134.
2   Holy Bible: New King James Version (New York, NY: American Bible Society, 1999).

Session 4
Transformed: From Dissatisfied to Content

💡 Day 1
Enlisted to Expose the Darkness

Do you or anyone you know suffer from what I call the "if only syndrome"? These two words can be found at the beginning of any discontented thought. *If only* my husband would help out more. *If only* I had more money. *If only* I had gotten that job promotion. *If only* the church would change its worship style. *If only* I were more attractive. *If only* I were taller. *If only* I didn't have to work full time. You think *if only* things were different, *then* you would have your happily ever after. Charles Spurgeon said it this way:

> *"You say, 'If I had a little more, I should be very satisfied.' You make a mistake. If you are not content with what you have, you would not be satisfied if it were doubled."*[1]

These *if only* thoughts are dangerous because they make you feel dissatisfied, jealous, and deprived. Entertaining these thoughts cause us to search for "satisfaction guarantees" found in products, programs, and propaganda. However, the satisfaction that comes from this world will only temporarily satiate our desires, and we soon find ourselves spinning our wheels as we strive to meet our unfulfilled desires.

C. S. Lewis, in *The Screwtape Letters*, describes this phenomenon as one of Satan's most effective strategies. The premise of the book is a collection of 31 letters, written by a senior demon named Screwtape to Wormwood, a less experienced demon, about how to mislead the human to whom he is assigned away from devotion to God. Here is an excerpt from letter 15:

> *"Our business is to get them away from the eternal, and from the Present….In a word, the Future is, of all things, the thing least like eternity….Hence nearly all vices are rooted in the future…Gratitude looks to the past and love to the present; fear, greed, lust, and ambition look ahead…we want a whole race perpetually in pursuit of the rainbow's end, never honest, nor kind, nor happy now…."*[2]

This strategy of the enemy to shift our focus off of God and onto what we lack in our present circumstances affects our thinking, which affects our outlook, which affects our posture, which affects our mood, which in turn affects our responses/actions. Focusing on the negative causes us not to see the positive.

For example, one day as I was getting my youngest daughter, then a toddler, ready to leave the house for an appointment. Every time I tried to hurry her along, I felt like she moved more slowly. Finally, I corralled her outside but she walked straight past the car and out of the garage onto the driveway. Before I said anything in my frustration, she turned to me excitedly and said, "Mommy, look at the sun, isn't it glorious! Look at the trees, they're dancing with the wind."

Tears filled my eyes. My negative lenses had prevented me from seeing the positive, though beauty was right in front of me.

God used my precious girl to shift my focus back onto Him that day, and I'm forever grateful. While the enemy tries to breed dissatisfaction, God promises that He *"will meet all your needs according to the riches of His glory in Christ Jesus"* (Philippians 4:9 NIV). God promises us over and over again in Scripture that He will satisfy not in some ways but in all ways and from His unlimited resources no less. When a sea of *if onlys* threatens to overtake you, instead of struggling to tread water, rest on the promises of God, be satisfied in Him, and allow Him to supply all your needs.

Engage with God

o   What *if onlys* fan the flames of discontentment in your thought life?

o   What might God be offering you that your lenses make hard to see?

o   How do lies and fear keep you trapped in a dissatisfied state?

Enabled through Spiritual Practice

When we feel weighed down by difficult people, circumstances, or decisions we can't control, it's easy to feel powerless to change anything and allow disgruntled thoughts to take center stage. While we may not be able to change our difficulties, we can change our perspective. When we stop and take time to thank God for who He is and what He has done, our focus shifts, changing our perspective even if our circumstances do not. When negative thinking clouds roll in, try gratitude and watch them dissipate.

Webster's dictionary defines *gratitude* as "the state of being grateful."[3] Gratitude, therefore, is more than just being grateful to God, but it implies a way of being or a mindset of gratitude. The discipline of gratitude trains the mind to live in a state of active thankfulness and appreciation of not only what God has done but is doing. If you can look at the reality of your present and find a way to be grateful to God for it, it may not change your circumstances, but I know it will change you.

Take some time to begin a gratitude list. What are you thankful for? Ask the Lord to stir your heart and begin writing. This is a list that never needs to end, and it can look different every single day. Try adding to this list every day and see if you are thinking or feeling different at the end of the week. Record what you learn. Remember, praise and thanksgiving turn us back to God, and a thankful heart is a contented one.

Day 2
Entangled by Sin

Ever heard of what psychologists call the comparison trap? It's a process that constantly compares by assessing and reassessing what one has or lacks as compared to what others have or lack. With each head-to-head challenge, we either end up on top, smiling slightly as we soak in our fleeting satisfaction, or we're in the loser's circle, finding ourselves feeling less than or rejected, kindling the flames of restless desires unmet.

Social media is one of the front runners in leading us into the comparison trap. Multiple times a day we are barraged by digitally retouched images conveying others' best moments, which we are then encouraged to rate with our "like" button and perhaps add our two cents in the comments section. This whole process makes us feel less than and cultivates jealousy, gossip, idolatry, division, dissatisfaction, and other fleshy desires as described in Galatians 5:20. Social media is likely here to stay, so to avoid the comparison trap, be aware of its pitfalls.

Paints an unrealistic picture. The way we define beauty is greatly influenced by the media. The images we see in magazines, on billboards, online, etc. shape our perceptions of what is beautiful, especially when it comes to our bodies. Rare is the image that isn't digitally altered, creating an ideal for beauty that can only exist with the help of a computer program. We are bombarded daily by hundreds of images like this, which makes it difficult to not compare ourselves and remember that the images are fake. The diet industry preys on our body insecurities and profits roughly $60 billion dollars a year in the United States alone as we strive to make ourselves fit this fabricated body ideal. Boost your body image by guarding your heart and mind by limiting your exposure to media that causes you to feel less than. God's design is so much better! Wouldn't the world be a boring place if we all looked the same? It's mind boggling to think about God's creativity and how He has managed to make over 7 billion people look differently. Let's use our energy to rejoice in what God made instead of wishing it was different.

Reduces space from social pressures. Another part of the problem is how much more access we have to those kinds of images and to each other on social media. It used to be that catching up with someone happened over the phone, at church or social gatherings, even by email. But now we have everyone's lives scrolling before our eyes on a live feed. Likewise, if a student drops their tray in the lunchroom, their embarrassing moment, while painful, will pass quickly and be forgotten in a day or two. They didn't have to worry about reliving the moment over and over again on social media, or worse yet, knowing their embarrassing moment was caught on video and went viral. We have fewer and fewer breaks from social pressures because our lives are now accessible and available for broadcast 24 hours a day like a reality TV show.

Cultivates unmet longings. What kinds of thoughts go through your mind while you're on social media? Are you are longing for your body to look more like hers, for your spouse to be more like him, for your boss to be more like your old one, for your house to be as nice as your neighbor's, or for your wardrobe ensemble to be more fashionable like hers? Whatever it may be, these thoughts often evoke feelings of discontentment. As we allow these thoughts to ruminate, they cause us to struggle to live in the present because we are either longing for the way things were or longing for things to be a certain way in the future. This grass-is-greener-on-the-other-side mentality leaves us feeling that if things were different, then and only then would we be able to rest in contentment.

Friend, discontentment harbors things and contentment unlocks things. When we live in a state of dissatisfaction with our lives, we harbor a breeding ground of discontentment, fear, anxiety, worry, unforgiveness, and bitterness. Whereas when we choose to be content in "all circumstances" (1 Thessalonians 5:18), we unlock and open the door of our hearts that allows God to sow and grow joy, hope, peace, faith, trust, and contentment in our lives.

I don't know about you, but being content in all circumstances seems like a pretty tall order. How can you switch your focus? Praise. As the battle rages in your mind, use thanksgiving as one of your weapons of warfare. When you praise God and thank Him for who He is despite what you are going through, your focus can't remain fixed on what you lack. This leaves us with a daily choice: continue in the comparison trap that leaves us restless, filled with anxiety and despair. No thanks. Or, concentrate our energy on our unchanging, sovereign, Almighty God. Our circumstances don't define us, God does. When trouble comes, let's join together and stand firmly on the promises that God has given us and remind each other of who we are: fearfully and wonderfully made, precious masterpieces, chosen daughters of the King.

I challenge you to try a radical approach of daily turning over your longings for bigger (or smaller), for better, or for more. Allow God to transform the lenses of dissatisfaction to new lenses of contentment so that you can trust that what He has for you is good. I challenge you to relinquish to the Lord whatever you are on the verge of complaining about today and *learn to be content whatever the circumstances"* (Philippians 4:11 NIV), unlocking all God has for you.

Engage with God

o   Do you struggle with falling into the comparison trap? Ask the Lord to reveal to you different situations that are causing your hang-ups.

o   What are some safeguards you could put into daily practice to avoid comparing yourself with others?

Enabled through Spiritual Practice

As the digital age continues, more and more research is being done to understand the effects of social media. There is already clinical evidence that directly connects low self-esteem, depression, anxiety, and body dissatisfaction with social media use. New studies are examining how technology negatively impacts the adult brain and the developing brain of children. Even after I gave a presentation to a roomful of teenagers last month about the potential risks and pitfalls of social media, in a follow-up survey they still reported they were on social media greater than ten times a day.

In order to counteract the negative impact social media can have, try gratitude through worship. Thanksgiving and praise are weapons of warfare. Next time you are feeling stuck in negative thinking, put on some of your favorite praise music, turn up the volume, sing loud, dance or do whatever the Spirit moves you to do and worship the Lord in song. Record your thoughts, how your body feels, your emotions before and after, and take note of what's changed. Perhaps create playlists of songs that help you refocus that you can use whenever needed.

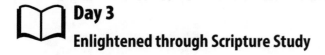

Day 3
Enlightened through Scripture Study

Pray

Lord, I confess all the ways that I struggle with being discontent. I'm sorry for how I compare what You have given me with what You have given to others. I'm sorry for how I long to have what others have and how sometimes I feel like You are withholding things from me. Show me the keys that will open ways to find contentment in You. Help me to thank You in all circumstances (1 Thessalonians 5:18). In Jesus' name I pray, amen.

Observe

Passage: Exodus 16 (NIV)

Understanding the context of a passage is vital to understand what the passage is saying. Today's text is long, but it is helpful to read the entire chapter so you can get a feel for what is happening in the story.

- o   This narrative is a part of a larger story. Describe briefly the context of what is happening.
- o   Cross references can also help us understand context. Read Psalm 106:7-15. Record what you learn.

Within the passage, repeated words and phrases used in a text signal the reader to pay attention because it is important enough to mention more than once. As you read through Exodus 16, look for repeated words and phrases.

- o   Be sure to mark the word grumble and its synonyms.
- o   Look up the definition for the word grumble. Record what you learn.
- o   Make a list with two columns; on the left write what the Israelites were grumbling about, and on the right describe God's response. Be sure to indicate the verse in which you found it.

Interpret

It is alarming how quickly the Israelites began complaining after God had miraculously set them free from slavery in Egypt. How does God show His lovingkindness to the Israelites despite their grumbling?

- o   Referring back to your list, what do you learn about God from His responses? List any attributes (character traits) of God that are evident in the passage.
- o   Thank Him for who He is using the attributes you discovered.

Apply/Engage with God

Take a moment to reflect on what you learned.

- o   Are there any ways you are romanticizing the past like Israel did, breeding discontentment in your heart?

- o   How does knowing that God still showed lovingkindness to the Israelites despite their grumbling change your view of God or yourself?

- o   What other truths might God be asking you to apply to your daily life?

Enabled through Spiritual Practice

As a part of our Scripture study, you worked on identifying attributes of God. Practice "alphabet prayer" to focus on the truth of who God is. Try and pray an attribute of God with each corresponding letter of the alphabet. For example: God you are the **A**ncient of Days (or **A**lmighty or **A**uthor), the **B**eginning (**B**enevolent or **B**anner), our **C**reator (**C**omforter or **C**ornerstone) and so on. It may seem awkward at first but with practice it will get easier. If you can't think of one, just keep going. The goal is worship, not perfection. Soak in the truths of who God is and rejoice in them as the attributes are prayed.

You can pray this way on your own or with a group. You can do this in written form, silently in your head, or out loud. When doing it with a group, go around the circle and have each person say an attribute of God with their corresponding letter. If someone cannot think of a word, don't stress, just say, "Praise you, Lord" which will cue the next person to go. Go through the alphabet as many times as you like. Afterwards, discuss if and how your attitudes or perceptions changed.

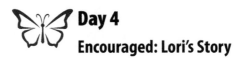

Day 4
Encouraged: Lori's Story

My eating disorder is only a response. Its core is much more profound. My life was ugly, for I was a child of poverty, alcoholism, emotional dysfunction, incestuous sexual abuse, and divorce. Hope was something not meant for me. With all the depression and despair, I found food made me feel good, and it comforted me in my life of turmoil. Even though it was comforting, I still found that I was not happy with myself or anything else.

As my self-esteem lowered as I matured, I became overweight in high school. The addiction to food expanded into cigarettes, alcohol, marijuana, and other drugs…and then sexual addiction as well. I was searching for contentment…peace…and I couldn't find it. I had no self-care tools to help me overcome and didn't want any. As far as I was concerned, I wasn't worth it. I came from the gutter and that's where I would always be. Daily survival was all I focused on. I would do what I needed to escape my life. Escape meant a perceived freedom that really became more imprisonment in my addictions.

In a rare moment of reaching out, I became a Christian at the age of nine or ten. My family wasn't Christian and didn't attend church. I was embarrassed by that because it seemed to me that almost everyone went to church. It felt like a certain class of people went to church and lesser ones didn't. I did go with friends at times, but it was sporadic. As a teen, I attended a Catholic church on and off for about three years with my cousin. The services were in Latin and meant little to me, and I found it to be only ritualistic practices. The worship seemed forced and not real to me. Without the enthusiasm I needed, I left.

So, I didn't grow in my faith walk, but God was with me even when I didn't know it. The Holy Spirit lived in my child's heart, protecting and loving me. He was faithful even when I wasn't, which became often since I was looking for something real to believe in. As I think back on my life, I can see how God was active in my life. I am so thankful for His constant presence no matter how my life was going.

I met my first love in my junior year of high school. We married and hoped to live happily ever after. Although he was a Christian, he was raised in a dysfunctional home too, and we both suffered from addictions. Our family expanded with three children in the first five years of marriage. Instead of this being a happy time, things grew worse.

Becoming a mother helped me to decide to give up all drugs and alcohol. I still smoked and flirted with the eating addiction although I kept my weight in check. However, my husband's habits worsened, and it led to physical abuse. I could not tolerate this, and after eight years of marriage, we separated and divorced. The addictions overran our marriage and destroyed it.

This turmoil caused me to spiral back down in despair for three years, where I escaped through drugs and alcohol. It's what I knew would comfort me instantly. Living in a continual fog, I abandoned my kids numerous times and held on to constant shame and guilt. The pain was so much that I had to remain high to function at all. I did anything to not experience any more hurt. I ran spiritually and emotionally. I wanted peace and contentment back in my life but was looking in all the wrong places.

God brought a man into our lives who has been a saint (although he is not Christian). I married him, and he has been a good husband, provider, and father to my kids. I will always be grateful for this blessing.

My husband does struggle with food addictions. It is something we work on together. I have not drunk alcohol, smoked, or taken drugs for many years. On difficult days, depression and food addictions still haunt me. I still look for my life to be better, feeling discontent.

What has helped me turn that thinking around is getting back into God's Word through study and hearing others share their stories. This has greatly encouraged me. I realize that all my addictions, disorders, pains, and hurts can only be healed by God. I have hope that I will find harmony in my life once again. God does great things all the time.

Engage with God

○ What parts of Lori's story resonated with you?

○ How do comparisons contribute to your eating and body image struggles?

○ What might God be asking you to do differently to move from dissatisfied to content?

Enabled through Spiritual Practice

Perhaps finding things to be thankful for has been more difficult than you anticipated, and the negative thinking clouds have not yet lifted. Try starting out by telling God everything about how you feel: the good, the bad and the ugly. God can handle your honesty, and He delights when you share your heart with Him. If you need help getting started, turn to the Psalms. They are filled with songs of praise, lament, and everything in between. They put words onto emotions in heartfelt expression to God. I challenge you to read through the Psalms until you find one that truly resonates with your heart. Then read that Psalm every day, meditate on it, memorize it, sing about it, hide it in your heart so that even at night your heart would instruct you (Psalm 16:7). Repeat this practice as many times as needed. Take note of any change in your thoughts, perceptions and countenance. Since God's Word is alive and active, your Psalm may change as your circumstances change, because God may want to encourage your heart differently in different seasons.

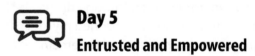 **Day 5**
Entrusted and Empowered

While we must beware of the dangers of social media, as discussed in Day 2, I want to challenge you to do three things in regard to your social media use to make it be more positive: change your filter, embrace the good, and effect change.

Change your filter. Before you begin scrolling through your daily feed, take a few moments to pray and ask God to change your filter. As you read about how your friend's making a difference with her nonprofit work, ask God to inspire you to impact others instead of telling yourself you're an underachiever who could never do something like that. As you look at photos of your friend's storybook wedding, ask God to help you celebrate with her instead of wondering how much longer you will have to wait for Mr. Right. As you learn about your aunt's latest marathon race, ask God to help you genuinely congratulate her accomplishment instead of telling yourself what a lazy slug you are. We have a choice every time we open our app as to how we are going to filter the information we take in. With God's help, we can approach our social media differently if we refuse to compare ourselves and focus on how we are less than. Remember to go before the throne before you go to your phone.

Embrace the good. Changing your filter releases you to embrace what's good about social media. First, it acts as a hub of connection. Family and friends who live in different cities, in different countries even, no longer have the same kinds of barriers of connection, which allows relationships to be rekindled, maintained, and strengthened. Second, it offers support. With the debut of online support groups, people struggling with similar issues—whether it be a physical malady, an eating disorder, or as victims of domestic violence—can support, encourage, and help each other without even living in the same city. Third, it offers increased access. With the click of a button, we can access a vast number of resources that can help us find information quickly and easily.

Effect change. Once you have changed your filter and embraced the good, I want to empower you to think of ways you can use social media as a mechanism to effect positive change in our society. Ephesians 4:29 says, *"Do not let any unwholesome talk come out of your mouths but only what is helpful for building others up according to their needs that it may benefit those who listen"* (NIV). What if we used our social media platform to build others up instead of tearing them down? What if the things we shared encouraged, affirmed, bolstered, appreciated, uplifted, and refreshed others? What if we used it to spread the good news of Jesus Christ and to point others back to Him? Make your next post, tweet, or pin kingdom minded. You never know what could go viral. It's worth a shot!

Engage with God

o   How does your social media use impact how you feel about yourself?

o   Write out some action steps you can take today to use social media to have a positive and uplifting impact on both you and others.

Enabled through Spiritual Practice

Take some time to reflect on the gratitude exercises you tried this week. Reflect on what was most helpful and what was the most challenging. Was there a particular exercise that helped to transform your thoughts and attitudes? Record what you learn. Ask God to help you highlight which one to apply into your daily life and start incorporating it today.

ENDNOTES

1   Charles Spurgeon, Available online at Crosswalk.com. 2 Nov 2015.
2   C. S. Lewis, The *Screwtape* Letters (New York, NY: Macmillan Publishing Company, 1959, 1982), 76-77.
3   "gratitude." Merriam-Webster.com. 2011. Online, 15 May 2019.

Session 5
Transformed: From Idolatrous to Devoted

Day 1
Enlisted to Expose the Darkness

When the topic of idolatry came up in one of my Bible studies, I thought I was finally going to be off the hook that week. I felt confident that I didn't struggle with idolatry because when I thought of it, my mind drifted to carved statues like those described in the Old Testament. It meant not worshipping God but something fashioned by man, and since I wasn't bowing down to any statues, I thought I was good. However, when author Beth Moore, stated that idolatry was, "ANYTHING we try to put in a place where God belongs,"[1] I felt like I had the wind knocked out of me. We weren't talking about carved statues anymore, and I realized in that moment that I was guilty of it, in fact, very guilty of it.

Further investigation of the word idolatry, led me to Webster's dictionary and the definition of reads this way:

> *Blind adoration or inappropriate devotion to something or someone holding illicit leverage or sway over decisions or priorities, time or resources.*[2]

Another blow. I sat back and reread the definition. Did I read it correctly? Inappropriate devotion to something or someone which holds illicit leverage over decisions, priorities, time or resources…yes, I had. I reluctantly asked God who or what was holding illicit leverage over my decisions, my priorities, my time, and my resources. I am aggrieved to say that the searching of my heart revealed that while God was on the list, He wasn't at the top. Oh no, I thought, how did I get here?

Maybe you're like me and are reeling with the recognition that God isn't on the throne of your heart. Be gentle with yourself. No one ever sets out to become idolatrous, just like no one ever sets out to have an eating disorder or become an alcoholic. Remember, God doesn't reveal sin in our lives to condemn us but to set us free (Romans 8:1-2). Instead, thank Him and begin the work of replacing whatever is on the throne of your heart with God alone.

Engage with God

o   Reread the definition of idolatry. Is there anything holding illicit leverage over you or to which you have inappropriate devotion?

o   Write about what you have allowed to become an idol in your life and reflect on how it became one.

Enabled through Spiritual Practice

Prayer walking can be a refreshing way to change up your prayer time. Some people find it easier to stay engaged with God while they are moving. Find a time to take a walk with Jesus this week. As you walk, tell God what is on your heart. Resist the urge to fill every moment with your own words and thoughts. Take time to listen for His voice and the creative ways He may be communicating with you.

Start your walk by asking God to show you what He desires you to know about how He is working in your life. As you review your last few days in your mind, reflect on what brought you joy or sorrow, what caused you to stumble or succeed, what things you need to confess or celebrate. Do any patterns emerge as you ask God what He might want to show you about yourself? As you pour out your heart to Him, ask the Holy Spirit's guidance in how to respond in healthy ways to what you learn.

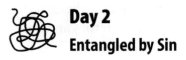

Day 2
Entangled by Sin

Once I got past the initial blow that God was not solely on the throne of my heart, I was able to start to look at what was competing for my devotion. Quite frankly, I didn't like what I saw. I had several offenders holding higher rank than God, one of which was people pleasing. All my decisions, my priorities, my time, and my resources were devoted to people first, not God. Keeping the people in my life happy seemed easier than dealing with conflict, disappointment, or failure. I was deceiving myself. I became preoccupied trying to meet their desires, not God's, and fear kept me entangled in a scenario I unknowingly created. But God did not put me here on earth to *"seek the favor of men…or strive to please them"* (Galatians 1:10) but to please Him and Him alone.

Not only was I looking to please others before God, I was also looking to them to rescue me too. Several years into my recovery, I relapsed. It was harder, darker, deeper than the first time around. I found myself looking to my doctor, my therapist, my dietician, my husband to rescue me. Who was going to be my knight in shining armor? Who would fix this and make me better? While they faithfully walked beside me every step of the way, they couldn't rescue me because that was God's job, not theirs.

Another repeat offender was an inappropriate devotion to food which held illicit leverage over my decisions, priorities, time, and resources. Every day I woke up preoccupied with how I would deal with feeling hungry—would I just ignore it or eat? Then I had to wrestle with what I was going to eat, when I was going to eat, how much I was going to eat, what people would say about what I ate, and then what I would say back. Then an onslaught of feelings of guilt quickly followed by urges to exercise, restrict, binge, or isolate would accompany any eating encounter. Maybe if I only ate items on my rather short but approved food item list, or maybe if I exercised a little more, then I could feel satisfied with my performance? On the other hand, maybe I should just give up even trying since I'd already fallen dreadfully short of my unachievable goal for the day…again. What started as inappropriate devotion now enslaved me. I had fallen prey to let my mind become *"set on earthly things"* with *"their god as their stomach"* (Philippians 3:19 NIV).

Satan was using an unhealthy relationship with food to trip me up. What I didn't realize was that God never intended for food to be a stumbling block, but instead He created it to be a blessing. God created our bodies to require energy, and He meets that need through His provision. The Garden of Eden paints a picture of lavish provision from God as He offered not only sustenance but also fellowship with Himself as Adam and Eve took delight in His creation. However, when Eve gave in to her cravings for forbidden fruit, her disobedience scorned God's blueprint for provision and broke her fellowship with God, causing her to hide in shame. I was unknowingly guilty of that because Satan had tricked me into believing that this alternate path had something better in store. Jesus said, *"Man shall not live on bread alone, but on every word that comes from the mouth of God"* (Matthew 4:4). Here, food is a symbol of God's provision to us. When our relationship with food becomes distorted, we find ourselves enslaved to another master. We are searching for provision from another means than God. Speaking from my experience of following this dead-end path, avoid it at all costs.

Another way of defining idolatry is based on the idea of putting your faith in something other than God. Maybe you're trying to fill those empty places in your heart with work, shopping, food, eating disorders, drugs, alcohol, promiscuity, self, others, your kids, your spouse, etc. I can testify that these things leave you unfulfilled and unsatisfied. God designed us to have empty spaces in our lives that are meant to be filled by God alone. He offers us streams of living water. He invites us to drink deeply from His eternal source. God wants us to know that He is enough and will fill our emptiness. It wasn't until I was in the loneliest and darkest places in my life that I discovered God truly is enough. When I recalibrated my list, placing God at the top, it changed everything.

Friend, idols can't rescue you, only God can. The psalmist says their idols *"are silver and gold, made by human hands. They have mouths but cannot speak, eyes, but cannot see. They have ears, but cannot hear, nor is there breath in their mouths. Those who make them will be like them, and so will all who trust in them"* (Psalm 135:15-18 NIV). Don't fall into this trap. Whatever you are using your time, energy, and resources to cultivate, you are allowing it to have mastery over you. Make God the object of your devotion. Don't wait until you are in your darkest hour; do it now! Let your depleted reservoirs be filled to overflowing by the One who can supply all your needs and takes delight in doing so.

Engage with God

o   What is holding inappropriate devotion in your life, and how is that affecting your relationship with God and others?

o   How do lies, fear, and dissatisfaction play a role in your inappropriate devotion?

o   Are you ready for a change? Take some time to ask the Lord to help you map out some steps you could take to implement some changes to remove the idols in your life.

Enabled through Spiritual Practice

While prayer walking can be a way to reflect on your own life, it can also be a way to cover a particular geographic place with prayer. Try prayer walking through your home. Take time to pray in each room of your house. Remove any idols that may be present there and pray for protection from their return. Be sure to take some time to listen in each room as well, asking God what He would want you to know. Pray for the people who will be in each room, for God to be present in their lives and for God to expose any idols in their lives.

Day 3
Enlightened through Scripture Study

Pray

Forgive me, Lord, for how I have allowed anything other than You to become an idol in my life. Teach me as I study today on how to remove the things I have tried to put in a place where only You belong. Show me what needs to change in order for You to reign on the throne of my heart. In Jesus' name I pray, amen.

Observe

Passage: 2 Kings 17:7-15, 32-41 (NLT)

Before studying the selected verses from 2 Kings 17, read the entire chapter. Understanding the context of the passage is crucial to grasping the meaning of the highlighted verses. It provides the necessary framework needed for you to begin your study.

Commands give us instructions about what we are to do or not do.

- o   Mark and then make a list of all the commands or instructions given to us from the Lord and record the verse number.
- o   Did the people obey God's commands? Make a list of how they responded to God in their hearts and in their actions.

Interpret

Reading Scripture in different translations can offer us new insight into the meaning of God's Word.

- o   Try reading verse 15 in as many different Bible translations as possible. Record anything new you learn about idols/idolatry and Israel.
- o   Which translation spoke most deeply to your heart and why? Record what you learned.
- o   Look up Revelation 3:16 and Matthew 6:24. How do these cross references shed new light on the passage?

Apply/Engage with God

In verse 9 it says, *"The people of Israel had also secretly done many things that were not pleasing to the Lord their God."*

o   Are you doing anything in secret that is not pleasing to the Lord?

o   How does secrecy play a role in keeping idolatrous habits around?

In verse 41, it says, *"So while these new residents worshiped the Lord, they also worshiped their idols."*

o   Are you worshiping the Lord and your own idols at the same time?

God says you can't do both. He is asking you to worship Him alone. Nothing is hidden from the Lord. Ask Him to cleanse you of any devoted things of your heart so you can be free from idolatry.

Enabled through Spiritual Practice

Wherever you like to walk, try praying through and over that space. If you are walking in your neighborhood, pray for your neighbors. If you are walking in a gym, pray for the people who frequent that establishment. If you are walking in a mall, pray for the people who are shopping and working there that day. If you are walking in a hospital, pray for the patients' healing and for the doctors and nurses who are treating them. This can be a one-time occurrence or an ongoing commitment. Afterwards, write about your experience.

 **Day 4**
Encouraged: Julia's Story

I'm not sure exactly when or how my eating disorder started, but I do know one thing: it was my idol, and I looked to it for salvation.

Early on, I sought salvation from loneliness and rejection. In elementary and middle school, the friends I thought I had often abandoned me, leaving me discouraged and dejected. But instead of seeking the Lord in my depression, I turned to an idol, my eating disorder. Since I had no power over the actions of others, I found comfort in controlling what I could: my lifestyle. I worshiped my newfound control through excessive exercise routines and restricted eating schedules. I poured everything I had into the idol I built, leaving little time left for family or serving others.

And then God got my attention. During eighth grade Bible class, He convicted me of my idolatry, and I realized I could not serve both Him and the eating disorder. I had been fixating on myself, my body, and my control, when I should have been focusing on God. But for several years, I couldn't bring myself to give up the eating disorder. During this time, I sought salvation from anxiety, self-hatred, loneliness, and rejection. Sometimes I would pray about these issues, but predominantly, I looked to false gods for help. I continued to worship my control over my eating, my identity of being thin, and the security of following all the eating disorder rules.

But idols cannot save. Eventually, I realized mine was actually destroying me. This chapter of my life begins my freshman year of college, when I was finally liberated from the constraints of my parent's supervision. With this newfound freedom, I ate less. Concerned by my drop in weight, the athletic director at my college eventually mandated that I get treatment at a residential treatment facility if I was to keep my scholarship. I was there ten weeks, and it was the most invasive treatment I had yet received. I graduated from the program feeling disgusted with my new body, betrayed by my college, and angry at God. My only hope was to transfer schools, thereby escaping the monitoring so I could lose weight.

After leaving my first college, I took the following semester off. This was my chance. My opportunity to regain control and take back the body I longed for. Under the most stringent self-imposed diet restrictions yet, I lost weight quickly. But my idol worship left me feeling empty. In fact, I was miserable. Fatigued, depressed, and forever-hungry, I stumbled towards a goal that was always just out of reach. The control I worshiped was an illusion, as was "the perfect body." Fear shackled me on my grave-bound journey; I could not forsake my anorexic lifestyle even though I wanted to. I began experiencing heart palpitations, which started out subtle, then increased in duration and frequency as the weeks wore on. I had heard of anorexics dying of heart failure and the thought terrified me. I hate to admit it, but this was the end I deserved. The punishment for sin is death. How fitting that my idolatry itself would be the agent of my destruction.

But God.

One night, when fear and sorrow threatened to overtake me, God spoke to me. I know the thoughts were from Him, because they were unlike any of the self-centered ones that had filled my mind the past few months. I didn't deserve to hear from Him, lifted from my pit, or to be healed, but that is exactly what God did. He gave me a new purpose that night. He called me on a path to new life. In the months to come, I found life in the death of my control. I found unspeakable joy in serving my Savior, my Defender, my Lord, and Creator. I was made to worship, but not to worship myself. I was created to worship the One who is worthy.

As I began surrendering my eating, exercising, and body to the Lord, my eyes were opened to see the eating disorder's claims for what they were: lies. I could never find the joy and peace I was longing for by worshiping my body and my control. Instead, I discovered they come from serving God. I experienced freedom from anxiety I had never thought possible. I used to believe that the eating disorder's fear-driven rules would hold me captive the rest of my days, but one by one, they fell away in the months that followed. I now served a new Master. One who had saved me by His grace, whose ways are good, whose words are life, and who holds power and authority over all false gods. What a God to serve; what a God to worship!

Today, God continues to help me live in recovery by reminding me of my purpose to worship Him, and the consequences of idolatry. He calls me to serve Him by encouraging others, even those who are struggling with eating disorders. I cannot do this if I am bogged down in my own. He calls me to my current job, which can be mentally, emotionally, and physically taxing. I cannot do this if the eating disorder is consuming my energy and strength. Not only is idolatry a grievous sin against the Almighty, but it also destroys one's life, and prevents one from experiencing the joy and peace of worshiping God. An idol cannot see, hear, or bring salvation. We were called to higher worship. Not to worship created things, but the One who is all-powerful, loving, and mighty to save!

Engage with God

o   How does idolatry contribute to your eating and body image issues?

o   What parts of Julia's story resonated with you and what will you do as a result?

o   What might God be asking you to do differently to remove idols in your life?

Enabled through Spiritual Practice

If prayer walking is a struggle for you, try doing it with a friend. Schedule a time to prayer walk with another believer. You could walk in a park, at your workplace, in your neighborhood. Pray for the people that play, work, or live in that space. Pray for their salvation, health, and families. Spend some time praying for each other's needs and requests as well. Jesus says, *"For where two or three gather in my name, there am I with them"* (Matthew 18:20 NIV). Enjoy the sweet communion in the presence of God together. Afterwards, write about your experience.

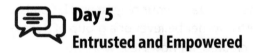

Day 5
Entrusted and Empowered

Hosea 14 beautifully describes how God will treat you as you give up your idols and worship Him alone. Friend, God is calling you to return to Him, to place Him on the throne of your heart. Confess to God the error of your ways and return to Him. He will forgive you and welcome you back with open arms. God doesn't stop there. He promises to heal you, refresh you, plant deep roots, and cause you to flourish in His shade. Pray this passage adapted from Hosea 14 based on the New Living Translation out loud over yourself, inserting your name in the blanks. Allow these truths to saturate your mind, body, and soul.

> *Return (insert name), to the LORD your God, for your sins have brought you down. Bring your confessions and return to the LORD. Say to Him, 'Forgive all my sins and graciously receive me so that I may offer you my praises. (insert idol) cannot save me, nor can our warhorses. Never again will I say to the idols I've made, 'You are my gods.' No in you alone do I find mercy.*
>
> *The LORD says, "Then I will heal you (insert name) of your faithlessness; My love will know no bounds, for my anger will be gone forever. I will be to (insert name) like a refreshing dew from heaven. (insert name) will blossom like the lily; it will send roots deep into the soil like the cedars in Lebanon. Its branches will spread out like beautiful olive trees, as fragrant as the cedars of Lebanon. (insert name) will again live under My shade. (insert name) will flourish like grain and blossom like grapevines. (insert name) will be as fragrant as the wines of Lebanon.*

O, (insert name), stay away from idols! I am the one who answers your prayers and cares for you. I am like a tree that is always green; all your fruit (insert name) comes from me. Let those who are wise understand these things. Let those with discernment listen carefully. The paths of the LORD are true and right, and righteous people like (insert name) live by walking in them. But in those paths sinner stumble and fall.

Engage with God

o   How did it feel to speak those truths over yourself?

o   How could you refresh and encourage someone else with the truths that God has entrusted to you this week?

Enabled through Spiritual Practice

Another thing to try on your prayer walk is praise. If you can walk outside, soak in God's creation and praise Him for the beauty He created. Another thing to try is praising God for whatever you see, for its beauty, usefulness, purpose. If you like music, get out your headphones, cue up your playlist and let praise be on your mind with each step you take. You could also do this with another believer or a group of believers as you walk together and praise God for who He is, for what He created, for how He is working.

If you struggle with the number on the scale being an idol, praise God by smashing your scale to symbolize the removal of this idol in your life. I pray that destroying it will destroy your bondage to it. And smashing it feels amazing, just saying…

ENDNOTES

1   Beth Moore, *Breaking Free: Making Liberty in Christ a Reality in Life* (Nashville, TN: LifeWay Press, 1999), 61.
2   "idolatry." Merriam-Webster.com. 2011. Online, 15 May 2019.

Day 1
Enlisted to Expose the Darkness

As a recovering perfectionist, I asked myself, why do I get so caught up in being perfect? While I recognize perfection is impossible, there is still something deep inside me that fuels my desire to achieve it. I began to wonder where this notion came from. Surely it is a godly pursuit, isn't it? I recalled one of Jesus commands from the Sermon on the Mount, *"Be perfect, therefore, as your Heavenly Father is perfect"* (Matthew 5:48 NIV) and reassured myself that while perfection was a tall order, I was still on the right track. However, further study of this verse brought new understanding.

First, I looked up the dictionary definition of perfect. Webster's defined it as "free from any flaw, fault or defect in condition or quality and complete." Second, I looked up the Greek definition of the word perfect, *teleios*,[1] which means the condition something is in, or describes the completion or end of, and maturity. Third, I looked up the cross reference for this verse and discovered Leviticus 19:2, which commands Israel to *"be holy because I, the LORD your God, am holy"* (NIV) using the word holy instead of perfect. Suddenly, I realized that this idea of perfect is talking about holiness and maturity, not about being flawless or acceptable.

This changes everything.

I had perfection as the goal, and I was failing miserably. But perfection isn't the goal, God is. The pursuit is about holiness and growing in maturity in my walk with God, not about whether I did everything perfectly. You see, God doesn't call us to pursue perfection, He calls us to pursue Him.

While pursuing perfection is one thing, striving for it is another. When we take the pursuit of perfection and place it on the throne of our heart rather than God, we stray off course and perfectionism becomes our ideology. Webster's defines this ideology as "a refusal to accept any standard short of perfection. A doctrine holding that religious, moral, social, or political perfection is attainable." If we adhere to this doctrine, pursuing perfection becomes the object of our worship, not God. Join me in shifting our focus off perfection and onto God, allowing Him to do the work of perfecting and maturing our faith whether it looks perfect to us or not.

Engage with God

o   In what ways do you struggle with perfectionism?

o   Is pursuing perfection an idol in your life?

Enabled through Spiritual Practice

We live in a world that is always striving for more. That equates to the accumulation of more things, squeezing one more thing into your schedule, and adding more work to get more money. "More" makes our lives even more complicated, often causing more problems. We soon realize that there are things that need to be eradicated from our thought patterns, our lives, and even our closets. Consider the practice of simplicity. The discipline of simplicity is defined this way: "Simplicity cultivates the great art of letting go. Simplicity aims at loosening inordinate attachment to owning and having. Simplicity brings freedom and with it, generosity."[2]

Simplicity has become a lost art. The ancients practiced simplicity, and while we may crave it, many have no idea how to do it. Try spending some time prayerfully examining the ways you spend your time, energy, thought life, and resources. After you've taken inventory, ask the Lord what areas need to be simplified. Then work on implementing a tangible step to simplify these different areas. We will also work through some areas together each day this week.

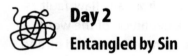

Day 2
Entangled by Sin

Before God showed me my misconceptions about perfection, it entangled every aspect of my life. This pursuit of being perfect launched me into a vicious cycle that evoked feelings of failure, frustration, inadequacy, unworthiness, and despair. As these feelings gained momentum, I found myself overanalyzing and ruminating on what I could have done better, fighting urges to retreat or isolate myself, and grasping for coping mechanisms to numb my feelings. I got caught up in being the perfect wife and mother with the perfect body, the perfect house, the perfect career, and the perfect kids in order to be loved, accepted, and worthy to walk on this planet. Can you relate?

Perfectionism is an unattainable illusion, and those who seek perfection will find themselves unfulfilled their whole lives. When we get stuck in that vicious, life-draining rat race of perfection at any cost, we need to remember who God says we are: beloved, forgiven, redeemed, chosen, loved, holy, accepted, precious, a masterpiece, and worth dying for…(just like we studied in session 1).

So why are we so caught up in being perfect?

First, it feels measurable. All day long we are compiling information about how we are measuring up and then recording our successes or failures on our mental spreadsheet of perfection. This process gives the illusion that acquiring more checkmarks in the success column directly correlates to our value, our worth, our significance. In the kingdom of God, our value is not based on our good works. *"For it is by grace you have been saved through faith. And this is not your own doing, it is the gift of God, not a result of works so that no one may boast"* (Ephesians 2:8-9 ESV).[3] Friend, Jesus Christ deleted your virtual spreadsheet when He died on the cross for you. It doesn't matter how you think you measured up today, God's love and grace for you are immeasurable.

Second, because perfect is the persona we think will lead to greater love, acceptance, and approval.
We think if my house décor looks like it came straight out of a Pottery Barn catalog, if there are fresh
vacuum streaks in my carpet, if I send my kids to school with sandwiches cut into animal shapes, and if
basically all parts of my life look Pinterest worthy, then surely I will be loved, accepted, and happy. Ask
yourself why you feel the need to present this perfect persona? Is it to gain praise and acceptance from
others? Or, is it to hide your pain? Whatever the reason, God says, *"Be careful not to practice your righteousness in front of others to be seen by them"* (Matthew 6:1 NIV). Presenting a mirage of having it all together
may give us a moment in the spotlight, but it doesn't sustain us. The reality is our mask of perfection is
stealing God's glory. We exist to bring God glory, not ourselves. The Bible doesn't say seek perfection and
be praised. It says, *"Seek first His kingdom and His righteousness"* (Matthew 6:33 NASB). If we can transfer
the energy used to be perfect to seek God first, we can trust Him to abundantly provide all we need.

Third, we want to author our own story. When we are the author, it gives us a sense of control. We de-
lude ourselves into thinking that things go better when we are in charge. However, Jesus is *"the author
and perfecter of faith"* (Hebrews 12:2 NASB), not us. The success of our marriages, our kids, or our careers
isn't riding on our ability to be perfect. Perfectionism swallows us up into the rat race of carrying the
weight of everyone's happiness, including our own, on our shoulders. While surrendering control to God
and trusting in His sovereign plan seems contradictory, it is here where you can find peace, freedom, and
rest. *"For I know the plans I have for you', declares the LORD, 'plans to prosper you and not to harm you, plans
to give you hope and a future"* (Jeremiah 29:11 NIV).

Life isn't perfect, and it never will be. It's messy. It's chaotic. It's unpredictable. Living focused on a futur-
istic unattainable goal is not a recipe for success. Instead, it highlights our weaknesses, intensifies our
failures, and leaves us unfulfilled. But Jesus said, *"'My grace is sufficient for you, for my power is made perfect
in your weakness.' Therefore, I will boast all the more gladly about my weaknesses, so that Christ's power may
rest on me"* (2 Corinthians 12:9 NIV). Did you catch that? Christ's power works best in our imperfections.

Beloved, what are you pursuing? Ask God to shine His light to expose your desire for perfection so that
you can see your imperfection as an opportunity for Christ to shine through you. It's time to remove the
veil of perfection and surrender our pursuit of it to the Lord. As we see through these new lenses, ask
God to transform your pursuit of perfection into a pursuit of Him.

Engage with God

o   Is your desire for perfection keeping you from being able to live in the present?

o   Is appearing perfect a stumbling block for you to see yourself as God sees you?

Enabled through Spiritual Practice

Simplify your time. Ask God to bring to mind that which He desires you to see regarding how you are spending your time and what changes He is asking you to make. Prayerfully consider these topics:

o *Your schedule:* Instead of feeling overwhelmed about where to start, try focusing on what you are lacking? Maybe it's time with God, maybe it's time with your family, maybe it's time with friends, maybe it's time for yourself, maybe it's time to exercise? Once identified, ask the Lord to show you what could be removed in order to make time for what is lacking.

o *Your priorities:* Once you have simplified your schedule, it's important to prioritize how you spend your time. What needs to change in order for you to have your priorities align with God's?

o *Your technology use:* Technology can be a time saver or a time waster. Are there any ways that your technology use can be changed so that it acts as a saver instead of a waster?

Prayerfully consider any changes God is asking you to make and try implementing them this week.

Day 3
Enlightened through Scripture Study

Pray

Lord, thank You that you don't call us to perfection but instead call us to pursue You. Remove the burden of perfectionism off my shoulders. Show me how to pursue things with eternal significance. Remove the veil of perfectionism from my eyes. Enlighten me through Your Word. Show me how to pursue You. In Jesus' name, amen.

Observe

Passage: 1 Samuel 16:1-13 (NASB)

When we ask questions, the answers give us the framework of what we are observing. Try asking these questions for the passage.

o Who is this story about?
o What is happening in the story?
o Where does the story take place?
o When does the story take place?
o Why is this story important?
o How does God choose the next king?

Interpret

Identifying the main characters of the story are important for understanding. Carefully mark all references to God and Samuel. Make a list of what you learn about the character of God and the character of Samuel. Use words from the text and record the verse number where the word is found for easy reference.

Apply/Engage with God

The second half of verse 7 says, *"The LORD does not look at the things people look at. People look at outward appearance, but the LORD looks at the heart"* (NIV). Considering our topic of perfectionism, how will you respond to God today knowing this truth?

- o   How does this change your expectations for yourself?

- o   Are there any changes you need to make in order to foster your internal qualities instead of your external ones?

Enabled through Spiritual Practice

Simplify your thought life. Cluttered minds whirring with thoughts and ideas can make us distracted, less productive, and anxious. Inner unrest steals our joy and peace by making it difficult to *"be still and know that [He] is God"* (Psalm 46:10 NIV). Consider emptying your mind of all its thoughts. Make lists of the things you need to do, journal your thoughts and feelings, or talk it out with God. Try visualizing your mind opening and all your thoughts pouring out into a bucket that Jesus is holding. Do whatever works for you. This may be a lengthy process but the peace that ensues is worth it.

Left unchecked, our thoughts can also lead us astray. 2 Corinthians 10:5 says, *"We destroy every proud obstacle that keeps people from knowing God. We capture their rebellious thoughts and teach them to obey Christ"* (NLT). Explore changes you may need to make in regard to what you're exposing yourself to, what you are meditating on, and what you are cultivating in your heart, so that, you can rein in those rebellious thoughts.

Ask God to bring to mind that which He desires you to see about your thought life. Pick one thing you can implement today to declutter your mind and heart, allowing more room for God. Record what you learn.

 **Day 4**
Encouraged: Chloe's Story

His hand slammed on the kitchen table making me jump. "These are the grades of a loser!" He dropped my report card. "Chloe, you can do better than this. Sure, there's a B here and there, but you should have all A's. You're not working hard enough. Stop being lazy and do it right!"

This scene represents a lifelong struggle of not being good enough...ever. My father was physically, verbally, and emotionally abusive at his worst; he was critical and manipulative at his best. To "pacify" him, my siblings and I had to be our very best at all times, or it was like a volcano waiting for his eruption.

In his manipulation, he either raged at imperfection that often turned to abuse, or false adoration that masked a request that required something from me that I was too young to realize was wrong. I thought that was normal for everyone, and I didn't question or despise it.

I learned well how to manipulate and used it on other people (not including the physical abuse). Basically, I was walking around on eggshells to not upset people, but letting my anger fly off the handle and always expecting people (especially men) who were nice to me to want something in return.

Not only did my father treat me this way, but my mother also would let me know that I didn't do anything right. My mom, a nurse, in her best attempt at teaching me nutrition, essentially nagged me that if I kept eating or not eating something, I would get fat. She felt the way I wore my hair and dressed would never attract a boy. She said I needed to look a certain way. I realize she was trying to help, but since I was used to being criticized at home, it made me feel like I was failing yet again.

There were two girls at my school that the boys considered gorgeous. They both had eating disorders. They were beautiful, athletic, and smart. I was nothing like them. I was a very late bloomer and uncomfortable with my body. I would eat lunch quickly so that I could leave. I would also hide in the locker room and inhale my lunch for I truly was very hungry. I didn't want to get caught eating like an animal.

The truth is that I used eating to handle my emotions. If I were sad, I would eat. The worry would seem to be lessened if I ate; eating made me happy and even celebratory at times. Somehow anger would make me not eat. This was either for my punishment or that of others. Then I would get very hungry and spin out of control.

Control made me feel safe. So, I wanted all the control I could get from others. I would manipulate them for control. When I was working and something wasn't going perfectly, I would refuse to eat or take a break. I believed the lie that if I failed, I would be rejected, fired, hated, and my reputation would be ruined. I used this tactic with those who I felt failed me. They would suffer from feeling responsible for my suffering. It was their fault I didn't take a break or eat. I was not a failure, they were. It was all a lie. I knew that taking a break would refresh my emotions and help me feel better, but I wanted the control more.

Subconsciously, I believed that once I achieved perfection, everyone would love me. I would be happy at last because everyone wanted me to do everything right. I know…crazy. Basically, I felt worthless. No one would ever love me. I felt I had to earn people's acceptance. So, people pleasing was my new way of control. I pleased people rather than looking to God to please Him. I was already accepted and loved by God, but I didn't believe it.

My unrealistic expectations of myself and others held me in a fist-like grip. People around me would either disappoint me or be overwhelmed, but I felt it was my duty to show everyone the right way of doing it. I lived without God and without grace.

Healing comes from God. In the last few years, I have experienced some of His healing in various ways. One way is that I found myself believing that anything that God made was beautiful. If I measured myself by worldly standards, I would lose every time. But with God I always win.

I also learned that controlling others was inappropriate and futile. Who did I think I was? I didn't have authority over them. I needed to focus on my own heart. My motives and behavior were not pleasing to

God. I am the temple of His Holy Spirit. God lives in me. I had to relearn self-care and add resting, eating healthy, and allowing God to show me the truth.

I learned about God's purpose for us in having food. It is a gift and blessing used to help me separate it from emotions. God's grace continues to help shape me in this journey with food. I will make it to the finish line with God's help.

Perfection is not realistic, so I have learned to let it go. The truth is that our bodies will not stay the same as we age. To pursue that is a waste and it will imprison a person to do it. This pursuit keeps out peace, joy, and love. Pursue what will not tarnish and is eternal.

Most of all, my pursuit of God allows Him to slowly grow, change, and strengthen me to be more like Him. Perfection will come at the pearly gates, but for now, I can rest in the truth that having God as my focus makes everything better. That's living in the best way possible. Perfectly loved and cared for. I am accepted.

Engage with God

o   What parts of Chloe's story resonated with you, and what will you do as a result?

o   How does perfectionism contribute to your eating and body image struggles?

Enabled through Spiritual Practice

Simplify your energies. God did not design us with an unlimited supply of energy, yet our performance-driven society is always pushing us for more. The demands of life can be exhausting. Plus, striving for perfection takes a lot of extra energy! You have already prayerfully evaluated your schedule and made changes. Now, assess what remains and determine what drains you and what fills you. Some assignments that drain you may need to stay in your schedule, but plan for time to recoup afterwards. Likewise, you may be able to do more of the things that fill you in one day than those that drain you.

Ask God to bring to mind the ways in which He desires you to spend your energy. Explore changes you may need to make in your expectations of yourself and others, who you are striving to please, the image you are hoping to portray, and what the cost is to you and your family. Ask God to help you formulate a schedule that will sustain your limited supply of energy throughout the week.

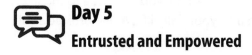

Day 5
Entrusted and Empowered

Becoming a woman of grace, contentment, faith, love, and peace are aspects of our character that are refined and matured over a period of many years, not days. If we try and sprint through this marathon, we'll end up burned out long before the finish line is in view. It takes perseverance to pursue God and a willingness to surrender to run the race He has mapped out for us, which often times doesn't feel very perfect. God knows what is best for us, and He responds kindly to our desires to pursue His narrow path.

Let me give you an example of what this might look like. Imagine a little girl running to her mother, brimming with delight and glee. With a big smile on her face, she thrusts her latest creation into the tender hands of her mother and says, "Mommy look what I made for you!" Would you expect the mother to frown with disapproval and say to her daughter, "This is terrible! You didn't even stay in the lines. Since when is a turtle purple? Look, you spelled your name wrong and some of the letters are backwards. How long is it going to take you to get that right?" No. Never. Wouldn't you respond positively and lovingly toward her heartfelt endeavor in creating a picture for you. Wouldn't you smile, celebrate her effort, thank her, and give her a big hug? Likewise, our heavenly Father responds to us with love, reassurance, and encouragement as we *"press on toward the goal to win the prize for which God has called me heavenward in Christ Jesus"* (Philippians 3:14).

Press on. Run the race. Learn from the detours. Accept the roadblocks. Entrust the race to Him. Allow Him to be the author and perfecter of your faith (Hebrews 12:2 NIV).

Engage with God

o   How differently would your life look if you pursued God instead of perfection?

o   You have learned that God is calling you to pursue Him and not perfection. How could you share this truth to refresh someone in your life this week?

Enabled through Spiritual Practice

Simplify your stuff. You already prayerfully decluttered your mind to create more peace and rest in your thought life. Decluttering your space is another way to bring tranquility to your life. Ask God if there are ways to simplify your stuff. Reorganize a closet or an area in your home. Sort through your clothes and give away what doesn't fit anymore. Donate things you don't use to a family in need. Getting started may seem overwhelming but giving just fifteen minutes a day to an area will make a sizable difference. Pick one thing you can implement today.

You have worked hard all week exploring with God how you can simplify your time and energy, thought life, and resources. Reflect on what changes you made and how they were helpful. Record how you feel and take note of any changes in your physical, emotional, or spiritual state. May you continue to incorporate the practices that were meaningful to you and adopt them into your daily life. A decluttered soul creates more room for you to be filled with more of God.

ENDNOTES
1   "teleios," Blue Letter Bible (online), cited 15 May 2019, Available on the Internet: *blueletterbible.com.*
2   Adele Ahlberg Calhoun, *Spiritual Disciplines Handbook; Practices that Transform Us* (InterVarsity Press, 2005), 74.

Day 1
Enlisted to Expose the Darkness

Love. From the beginning of time, man has sought it, experimented with it, and studied it in order to somehow solve its puzzle. It is so complex, the Greeks have not one, but eight different words to describe the many aspects of love, and some languages have almost as many as two dozen. Countless books have been written about love. How to get it, how to keep it, and what to do when you've lost it. But all of those books focus on you and what you need to do in order to be loved again. What if you didn't have to do anything? What if there was a love that was trustworthy, everlasting, and free to anyone who wanted it with no restrictions, no exceptions, and no conditions? Friend, this is the kind of love God offers you. God loves you because of who you are, not because of what you do. Not convinced? Let's look at some Scriptures together.

> *"For God so loved the world, He gave His only Son that whoever believes in Him will not perish but have everlasting life"* (John 3:16 NIV).
>
> *"Neither life nor death, neither angels nor demons, neither the present nor the future, nor any powers, neither height nor depth, nor anything else in all creation, will be able to separate us from the love of God that is in Christ Jesus our Lord"* (Romans 8:38-39 NIV).
>
> *"…The life of Christ will be released deep inside you, and the resting place of his love will become the very source and root of your life. Then you will be empowered to discover what every holy one experiences—the great magnitude of the astonishing love of Christ in all its dimensions. How deeply intimate and far reaching is his love! How enduring and inclusive it is! Endless love beyond measurement that transcends our understanding—this extravagant love pours into you until you are filled to overflowing with the fullness of God"* (Ephesians 3:17-19 TPT).[1]
>
> *"I have loved you with an everlasting love"* (Jeremiah 31:3 NIV).
>
> *"This is how God showed His love among us: He sent his one and only Son into the world that we might live through Him. This is love: not that we loved God, but that He loved us and sent His Son as an atoning sacrifice for our sins"* (1 John 4:9-10 NIV).

God's love sacrifices, surrounds, embodies, endures, includes, transcends, fills, satisfies, secures, is intimate, and endless. I know it sounds too good to be true, but it is true. God loves you because you are His child and He created you, not because of what you've done or not done. Worldly love cultivates a love that is self-focused that is constantly searching to replenish its supply through people, pleasure, and material things. However, these alternate sources don't satisfy. God's love is different. It's unlimited, unconditional, reliable because God is the source of love and nothing else. We are created with a longing only God can fill. Allow Him to satisfy your longings for love.

Engage with God

o Are you seeking love from a source other than God?

o Why is it so easy to forget how much God loves you?

Enabled through Spiritual Practice

We carry better technology in our pockets than was available to NASA when they sent man to the moon. Its chirps, rings, and buzzes beckon us to feast on the world's buffet of opinions, likes, politics, video games and the like. In a culture that routinely and consistently bombards our senses, meditation has become a lost art. In our increasingly "on demand" lifestyle, we have eliminated a lot of our down time which often acted as our think time. Nowadays, we don't talk, we text; we don't daydream, we scroll; we don't inquire, we google, making the discipline of meditation an atrophied muscle. Meditation requires slowing down, eliminating distractions, and focusing on one thing. When we meditate on Scripture, it allows us to shift from thinking "conformed to the world" and instead *"be transformed by the renewing of our minds"* (Romans 12:2 NIV). The world fills our minds, but truth transforms our minds.

This week try meditating on this verse from 1 John 4:10, *"This is love: not that we loved God, but that He loved us and sent His Son as an atoning sacrifice for our sins"* (NIV). I encourage you to find this verse in four or five different translations and read the verse both silently and aloud. Perhaps one translation spoke more to your heart than the others. Make this translation the focus of your meditation today. Then try your best to eliminate all distractions and clear your mind so that you concentrate on each word in this verse. Record any words or phrases the Holy Spirit highlighted for you as you meditated on this verse. If this exercise raised any questions, write them down and ponder them with the Lord.

 **Day 2**
Entangled by Sin

God created us with a need for love. As our relationships flourish with it and crumble without it, we long to know love's intricacies so we can have it in our lives and keep it. We spend much of our lives seeking to love and to be loved, but this search often leaves us empty and unfulfilled. It's often because we are "lookin' for love in all the wrong places" as country singer Johnny Lee sang. Because God is love (1 John 4:8), our need for love is satisfied in Him alone. I began to wonder, if it's that simple, then what keeps us from knowing and experiencing love?

Even though I had wonderful, loving parents, I spent my life under my own erroneous premise of needing to prove that I was worth having in order to be loved. My faulty logic from childhood told me that love was conditional and was given out in an "if/then" pattern. If I did what others wanted, then I would be loved. If I didn't, then I would be rejected and abandoned. Those fears of rejection and abandonment were so intense that I avoided them at all costs by becoming masterful at people pleasing in order to feel loved.

No matter how hard I tried, I failed to keep everyone around me happy, which to me meant I was a failure. Lies that I was a disappointment, unworthy, and unacceptable inside and out, grew louder and drowned out the truth that I knew. Taking matters into my own hands, I desperately searched for something I could do to make myself pleasing, acceptable, and worthy again. This distorted thought pattern helped give birth to my eating disorder. Don't be fooled by worldly alternatives that offer an appealing yet misguided shortcut to acceptance, love, and worthiness. They don't satisfy because only God's love can make you complete (1 John 4:17).

In order to heal, I had to identify and face my faulty perceptions.

No fear in love. Fear drove me to place high expectations on myself that were perfectionistic in nature—I thought fewer mistakes meant more security in my relationships. However, my heart's motive was approval seeking, not God pleasing. I was no better than the Pharisees who believed their strict adherence to external means of following religious law made them holy. I had fallen prey to a works-based methodology that said I could earn holiness, love, and acceptance. It is a hard way to live when your worthiness is based on others' approval. Because I looked to others for love, I was always afraid I wouldn't be loved. 1 John 4:18 says, *"There is no fear in love. But perfect love drives out fear, because fear has to do with punishment"* (NIV). Instead of turning to God with that fear and my need for love, I just worked harder at pleasing. I had to learn that God did not design love to be rooted in fear but rooted in Him.

Receiving love instead of striving for it. My ability, or lack thereof, to please others often left me feeling disappointed, abandoned, rejected, and alone. The problem was I was on a hamster wheel working my tail off in order to somehow guarantee that I would be loved. One day when I was feeling the weight of those feelings more intensely, I read Ephesians 2:8-9 about salvation, it says, *"Nothing we did could ever earn this salvation, for it was the gracious gift of God that brought us to Christ! So no one will ever be able to boast, for salvation is never a reward for good works or human striving."* (TPT) God used that verse to help expose my faulty thinking that I needed to earn love and prove I was worth loving. Salvation, which truly is God's most lavish expression of love to us, is a free gift offered to me and there is nothing I could do or strive to get it.

This new lens changed everything. It exposed the root of my problem: my inability to receive love. I couldn't receive God's love for me because I didn't view myself as lovable, at least the way I was currently. I kept striving to be someone else, because I struggled to accept that I was complete just how I was. God reminded me that while I couldn't be certain of others' love, I could be certain of His. However, 1 John 4:19 says, *"We love because He first loved us"* (NIV). When we can rest in God's love for us and accept ourselves how we are, it enables us to love ourselves and thus enables us to love others.

God is the source of unlimited and unconditional love. As humans our time, energy, and resources are limited, so of course I was often disappointed. I was drawing from a well that would run dry instead of drawing from God's unlimited well. My imperfect thinking had me looking to others as my source of love and placing my view of myself and my value in the hands of others. If I had their approval, then I was a good person worthy of love. If I didn't, then I was a horrible person and unworthy of love. Thankfully, God doesn't love us in "if/then" statements. God loves us unconditionally, which means His love is not earned, it just is. *"For God so loved the world that he gave his only Son, that whoever believes in him should not perish but have eternal life"* (John 3:16 NIV).

Did you catch that? God lavishes us with unmerited favor, sending His Only Son to die for us so that we could spend life eternally with Him *"while we were still sinners"* (Romans 5:8 NLT). If that wasn't enough, the Bible also tells us that *"nothing in all creation will ever be able to separate us from God's love"* (Romans 8:39 NLT). NOTHING! Embrace the truth that nothing can separate you from God, not even you. There is nothing you (or anyone else) could do—no mistake, no sin—that could prevent Him from showering you with His love. This revelation was mind-blowing for this recovering approval addict.

How I wish I could go back to my younger self and tell her, "You missed it! You don't have to do anything to earn God's love, its unconditional and you're enough just the way you are." Beloved, ask God to remove the idea that if you are pleasing, perfect, and sinless, then you are worthy. Let God transform your heart with His love so that you will be who He created you to be, not the "you" others want you to be. Know this: You are loved. Receive His unconditional love that He has promised you so that you can love yourself and those around you.

Love isn't supposed to hurt. Maybe you have trouble knowing what God's love is like because what you have endured in the name of love has been distorted, twisted, and painful. People who were supposed to love you instead hurt you, used you, betrayed you, divorced you, or abused you—emotionally, mentally, physically, sexually, spiritually. Maybe after all you've been through, you want nothing to do with love and feel more comfortable running and hiding your heart in order to protect it from being hurt again. Maybe you believe the way you were treated is your fault, like something is flawed in you, and you deserved to be treated this way. Friend, love isn't supposed to hurt.*

If this describes your earthly experience with love, I can only imagine how difficult it would be to trust and believe God's love is different. While neither you nor I can change your circumstances or rewrite your story, God can transform your future. God didn't design love to hurt us but to heal us. God loves you for who you are, not for who or what you or others think you should be. Remember the truth of God's Word from the Scriptures you read in session 1 that describe how you are His masterpiece (Ephesians 2:10 NLT), chosen (1 Peter 2:9 NIV), precious (Isaiah 43:4a NIV), redeemed (Ephesians 1:7 NIV), forgiven (Psalm 103:12), and fearfully and wonderfully made (Psalm 139:14). This is who you are. Defined by God, not by the world.

If this describes you, please tell someone and get the help you need. Situations like the ones described above are serious and complex and require professional help. Resources for victims of abuse can be found at leslievernick.com.

Engage with God

o   Do you feel worthy of God's love?

o   What will it take for you to be able to receive and accept God's love for you?

o   If you struggle with people pleasing, who do you struggle to please the most and why?

Enabled through Spiritual Practice

Incorporating memorization along with meditation can be a powerful tool. Psalm 119:11 says, *"I have hidden these words in my heart so that I might not sin against you"* (NIV). When we memorize Scripture, we plant God's Word deep with our memory, allowing Him to bring it to mind, to direct, to encourage, or to rebuke as needed. Memorization is also a way of meditating on a verse. The repetition keeps the verse at the forefront of our minds and allows us to process at different times of day, in different circumstances, in the midst of different emotions.

Try memorizing 1 John 4:10 in the translation of your choice. Help seal it into your heart and mind by repeating it out loud while standing, sitting, and lying down. Write it on a notecard to carry with you. Post it on your mirror. Make it your background on your phone. Make flashcards and have a friend quiz you. Put it to music. Do whatever works for you to cement this truth into the foundation of your being. Let the truth of God's Word permeate and saturate every aspect of your being as you mull over the profound truth of these words this week. I challenge you to continue doing this same exercise using other Scripture passages in the future and allow God's Word to lay a firm foundation in your heart.

Day 3
Enlightened through Scripture Study

Pray

Lord, forgive me for all the ways I have looked to others for love instead of You. Help me to accept that Your promise that You will never leave me nor forsake me (Deuteronomy 31:6 NIV). Give me a desire to seek You and only You to fill the empty spaces of my heart so that I may overflow with the love You placed there. In Jesus' name I pray, amen.

Observe

Passage: 1 John 4:7-21 (NIV)

When observing a passage, it is important to look for God and what we learn about Him.

Session 7

Read through the passage and mark every reference to God the Father, Jesus, and the Holy Spirit. Marking examples: for God I used a red triangle, for Jesus I use a red cross, for the Holy Spirit I encircle the words with a red cloud.

Using the repeated words tool, read through the passage again and mark the word *love* with a heart around it every time it appears. Make a list of every time it appears and what you learn about love.

Interpret

The word *love* appears more than two dozen times. Refer back to your list of what you learned about love.

- o   What do you learn about how God loves?
- o   What do you learn about how we are to love others?
- o   What does this tell us about God's character?

Apply/Engage with God

Read the passage again.

- o   What verse inspires you to love yourself the way God loves you? Research the verse in several different translations. Write out the one that resonates most with you and stick it around your house as a reminder throughout the week of how God loves you.

- o   What verse do you think describes how we can love others? Again, look up the verse in different translations and write out the verse. Based on what this verse describes, give an example of a way you could refresh others through God's love this week.

- o   How would your life look different if you believed in your heart that God knows you, finds you worthy, and loves you?

Enabled through Spiritual Practice

Today you were able to study 1 John 4:10 in the context of its surrounding verses. Understanding the cultural, historical, and overall context of a verse gives further insight into the meaning of the verse. The English word *context* is derived from two Latin words meaning "to weave threads."[2] As you read the entire chapter, look for how God is weaving the threads together into a greater tapestry of meaning of God's love for us.

Record anything new you learned from reading the verse in context and take some time to meditate on the new truths you gleaned. Ask God if there are any changes that need to be made in your thinking to allow you to accept the truth of this verse for yourself. Think about how you can implement those changes into your daily life.

Day 4
Encouraged: Naomi's Story

I wish I could pinpoint exactly how I ended up in this place. I mean, it's not like any child grows up dreaming of having an eating disorder, but yet here I am, and it seemed to just "happen." It has been an evolution with ebbs and flows, and I have learned a lot over the years, but ultimately, I am a work in progress. God is still leading me on this journey and will never give up on me…no matter what.

Growing up, I remember there was a lot of focus on nutrition and body image. My father was in the healthcare field and constantly had to point out the body habits and eating habits of anyone he saw… in the name of health, of course. He seemed to emphasize that those who were overweight were weak, undisciplined, and "less than." There were times at a very early age when I wanted a second helping of food or extra dinner roll but held back in fear that my father would point it out. I was the first-born child and was your stereotypical type-A, overachieving, perfectionist daughter.

Ironically, my mother was obese my whole life, and my father did not always hold his tongue about it. They deeply loved each other, but it created a strange disparity hearing them interact. Those memories stay in my mind, and I know they had an effect on my whole self-image.

Fast forward a few years through elementary school and middle school, and I am entering my freshman year of high school. Socially, I was struggling to fit into a particular group at school, and my personality led me to isolate and focus on excelling in sports and academics. I was always critiquing and dissatisfied with my body image, and I thought everything would be "magically" better if I were thinner. After all, it was instilled in me that "thin and fit" body types meant you were powerful, disciplined, and "better than." Thus, the eating disorder began.

I put lots of energy into watching fat grams and calories and remember times when I would bring a Slim-fast shake to school for my whole day. As the weight went down, I started feeling better and more empowered. However, this feeling was a cheap imposter and soon gave way to returning dissatisfaction and feeling empty inside. I was hiding this secret, which was exhausting and felt like I was having to "fake it" all the time.

My thoughts were constantly consumed with what I was eating/not eating, exercise, weight, body image, and performance critiques which drained me. I was drowning on the inside, but things looked great on the out. I became proficient at lying and hiding. When my parents started noticing my restriction with eating, I "out-fooled" them by eating meals in front of them but purging afterwards. This seemed to appease them for a while, and it wasn't until my senior year of high school that my parents became concerned with my weight loss and confronted me about the eating disorder.

Instead of compassion, I was met with very sterile and cold disappointment. They seemed to want me in treatment as soon as possible and just "get over this." In treatment, I only had one parent visit me once. They would not come to any of the family invitations and did not hide that they were skeptical about counseling and would not attend that either. I felt so alone and ashamed that my parents were "disappointed and embarrassed" by me. What I forgot was that my heavenly Father never sees me like that. He loves me unconditionally, and there is nothing I could ever do that would cause Him to turn His back on me. He was walking beside me every step; I was just ignoring Him.

I completed the program with some restored weight and eating, but I was not changed on the inside, so this was just a temporary external fix. In college, I withdrew and isolated even more. I shut most everyone out of my life, including my relationship with God. I focused heavily on academics, completing a pre-med degree in three years and getting accepted into multiple medical schools. Despite my achievements, I was miserable on the inside because my eating disorder thrived in this isolated and unchecked environment, but on the outside, I acted as if things couldn't be better.

I ended up getting married, graduating, and started working. I wasn't honest with anyone and became a professional at people pleasing and faking my true emotions, keeping that perfectionistic persona intact. I was physically and emotionally exhausted and something had to give. Anxiety and panic attacks came on a regular basis and eventually I got into counseling again. I was about to start on a medication when I discovered I was pregnant. This was a bit of a wake-up call and gave me the motivation to get the eating disorder behaviors in check; however, my mindset and spiritual life were still in disarray. I seemed to have an easier time than I expected with the weight gain and body changes, and once my daughter was born, she became my focus. I was not engaging in the eating disorder behaviors and seemed to truly accept and appreciate my body. For a year, it seemed that the eating disorder nightmare was finally behind me. I once again found out that I was pregnant, and life felt perfect. However, perfection is not possible and in my second trimester, I miscarried our precious child. I was devastated. In the pain and chaos, I turned to what I knew best to cope: the eating disorder.

To avoid the pain of my loss, I focused on what and when I would eat and not eat. I constantly critiqued my body image, especially with the hardship of having to lose the baby weight and baby bump with nothing to show for it. It was like a cruel joke. Things seemed to be spiraling downward again, but this time I was able to identify it a lot sooner and seek help. I realized that although I was able to fix behaviors, I needed to fix things on the inside and change some of my false beliefs and replace them with God's truth.

I had let my heart, soul, and mind wander away from my heavenly Father who had never asked me to be perfect, but to be His image bearer, seeking Him always. My inappropriate devotion to body image, perfectionism, people pleasing, and diet had consumed my thoughts and emotions, holding me captive. I was no longer able to hear what my Father said about me in His Word and could not see that He was calling me to surrender it all and rest in Him. God has and always will have a better plan than us; we just need to trust Him. The more I dive into the Lord's truth and meditate on His promises, I feel more free and content. I can't say that everything changed overnight. I'm still a work in progress and have a long way to go, but thank goodness our gracious God is in the business of broken people and loves us despite our flaws.

Engage with God

    o   What parts of Naomi's story resonated with you, and what will you do as a result?

    o   How does unworthiness contribute to your eating and body image struggles?

    o   What might God be asking you to do differently to receive His love?

Enabled through Spiritual Practice

Scripture meditation and memorization can bring transformation. If this practice has done that for you, I encourage you to share that testimony with someone else. We all have brokenness, sin, and hurt in our lives. Our natural tendency is to hide it out of fear and shame instead of allowing others to be comforted by it and grow from it. God can use our pain to help others walk through theirs. Will you let Him use yours?

You don't have to be "all put together" to testify. Just like Naomi testified about what God did in her life, you can also testify and celebrate what God has done in yours. Sharing your testimony is a spiritual discipline in that it teaches us how to look back and rightfully give God the glory for what He has done in our lives.

If you are doing this study with a group, take some time to share collectively and celebrate all that God has shown you, promised you, done for you, changed in you thus far. Bless others with a testimony and be blessed by theirs.

 **Day 5**
Entrusted and Empowered

Every day your body reminds you when you are hungry, thirsty, or tired, signaling a need to eat, drink, or sleep. I think oftentimes we recognize our physical needs more readily than our spiritual ones. When we respond to the signal of feeling empty inside, we more readily turn to physical things to fill that emptiness. Maybe you have been turning to food, exercise, friends, a spouse, shopping, social media, prescription drugs, or alcohol to fill your empty places. They may have offered you temporary satisfaction or fulfillment, but soon your body sent you the "I'm empty" signal again. So, what will you turn to fill your empty places when that internal signal goes off again?

Jesus describes in John 4 what He can offer the woman at the well who has tried to find love and fulfillment through men. He says, *"but whoever drinks the water I give them will never thirst. Indeed, the water I give them will become in them a spring of water welling up to eternal life"* (John 4:14 NIV). Jesus sees beyond her physical thirst and into the thirsting of her soul, her unquenched heart. He offers her living water (v13) that will quench her thirst forever. He describes the source of the water like a spring. That word spring can also be translated "fountain," giving us a picture that what Jesus is offering you will never run dry; it's never-ending, it is eternal. Even if you feel dry, God promises to make streams in the desert. Jesus is offering this living water to you too. Think about it—if you turn to God to fill you, then you don't have to seek out other sources to fill you up because He is the source.

Engage with God

o   What is keeping you from turning to God to satisfy all your longings?

o   What changes do you need to make to allow God to fill your empty places?

o   What can you do to share this truth with someone else?

Enabled through Spiritual Practice

You learned from 1 John 4, that out of God's love for us, we can love others. Cut out a large heart out of a piece of construction paper. Write down all the promises you gleaned from this week's study concerning God's love for you on the paper heart. May this heart be a tangible reminder of the truths you wrote on your heart this week through meditation and memorization. Tuck it into your Bible to serve as a reminder when you are tempted to please man rather than God. Remember, God is unchanging. He loved you yesterday. He loves you today. And He will love you tomorrow.

Sometimes it's hard to remember those truths when we are walking through the valley. Ask God if there is anything you could do differently to love and encourage other people in your life, to point them back to the one true source of love, God. I have a friend who often texts me the words "You are loved." What an encouragement and great reminder of the truth. Is there anyone in your life you could encourage in the same way?

ENDNOTES

1   Holy Bible: The Passion Translation (Savage, MN: Broadstreet Publishing Group, LLC, 2017).
2   R. Herbert as quoted in tacticalchristianity.org. Online 12 May 2019.

Transformed: From Prideful to Humble

Day 1
Enlisted to Expose the Darkness

When I thought of someone as prideful, I imagined an arrogant, boastful person with an ego so big that it left no space for anyone or anything else. That is until my pastor shared this definition of pride one Sunday morning:

> *Pride is thinking too much about yourself, either too highly or too lowly of yourself, and not enough about God.*[1]

Wait a minute. Thinking too lowly of yourself is also prideful? I audibly gasped. My head started spinning. Oh no! My mind often focused on thoughts of my failures, my unworthiness, my insecurities, and my shortcomings. Being full of myself was something I was confident I was not guilty of, but this…

I started to tune back into his sermon just as he was talking about how pride manifests itself in different forms, like comparisons, competition, mocking, blaming, ingratitude, bitterness, complaining, manipulation, outbursts of anger, revenge, defensiveness, lack of concern for others, despising authority, selfish ambition, harshness, impatience, perfectionism, and being judgmental.

Yikes! That is some kind of list. At first, I was frantically writing, but soon my pen stopped moving as I unfortunately found myself struggling with more categories than I wanted to admit. This new knowledge knocked me right off my prideful pedestal. Oh, how the truth hurts. Isn't that just like Satan to trick me into believing that I was succeeding in this area only to discover nothing could be farther from the truth.

Engage with God

o   What emotions did this new knowledge of the definition of pride stir you?

o   Prayerfully look back at the list of manifestations of pride. Which areas are a struggle for you and why?

Enabled through Spiritual Practice

Pride can make us turn to other things for rescue instead of God. For example, maybe you are turning to food or withholding food to numb your feelings? Maybe you are engaging in excessive exercise to feel some accomplishment in the midst of failures. Maybe you know you need help but are too proud to ask for it.

When there is nothing you can do to change your situation, it feels good to have something to do and gives you the illusion that you are changing things. But this isn't really the kind of change you want. You aren't getting the results you hoped for but maybe you know what to expect from these behaviors and that feels stabilizing. Friend, stop taking matters into your own hands to fix something that is out of your hands. That's rooted in pride and it's time to let it go.

Are you ready to let go and let God? Try using the method of palms down, palms up to release things to God, allowing Him to transform your heart and, in turn, change the kind of fruit you bear. Let's practice together. Take one of those areas you identified and imagine yourself holding it in your clenched fist with your fingers facing downward. As you pray, confess it to the Lord, and then physically release it to His capable hands by opening your fists. When you are ready, turn your palms upward as a symbol of your desire to receive from the Lord. Ask Him to replace it with what you need. Maybe it's a heart to trust Him more. Maybe it's peace instead of fear. Maybe it's accepting His plan for you. Listen and wait in silence for God to meet you and supply your need as you commune with Him. Allow God to write these truths on your heart, take root, and transform you to be more like Him.

 ## Day 2
Entangled by Sin

If pride is thinking too much about yourself, either too highly or too lowly and not enough about God, then what is humility? The word *humility* gives the impression of someone who is shy, seen but not heard, has a low view of themselves and, in essence, weak. No one wants to appear weak because that implies deficiency, shortcomings, and imperfection, which makes us feel vulnerable, inept, and powerless. Things we all try desperately to hide. But that is not what humility means. George MacDonald described it this way:

> *Humility is not thinking less of yourself, it's thinking of yourself less.*[2]

God gives us a method, a road map, for prosperity and success by having the Scriptures at the forefront of our thoughts and as the focus of our thoughts. You will think of yourself less when you *"keep this book of the law always on your lips; meditate on it day and night, so that you may be careful to do everything written in it. Then you will be prosperous and successful"* (Joshua 1:8 NIV). When we surrender our thoughts to God, it gives more real estate in our minds to Him. And when our thoughts dwell on our great and almighty God, it leaves little room for anything else and forces out our prideful inclinations.

Unfortunately, this does not just happen and requires some action on our part. Proverbs 4:23 says, *"Above all else, guard your heart, for everything you do flows from it"* (NIV). In order to guard our hearts and our minds from a prideful spirit, we must beware of potential open doors. We will explore three potential problem areas together.

Beware in whom you are confident. When our confidence lies in ourselves, we open the door to pride in two ways. First, because we are confident in our abilities, we have less of a need for God and do more in our own strength. Second, because we are confident in what we do, we can take matters into our own hands without consulting God, in essence conveying that we know better than God. These thought processes are indeed dangerous, often flying under the radar at a subconscious level. One would likely not say, "I know better than God," but the way we live our lives and the choices we make may convey otherwise.

Think of the parent/child relationship, for example. When a child is born, she relies on her parents to take care of her. In the early years, the child is eager to learn and looks to her parents to help her learn new skills. As the child grows older, the more skills she has learned means the less help she seeks from her parents. By the time the child is a teenager, she acts like she knows everything and doesn't need any help from her parents. Parents long to help their teens avoid the many dangers of our world and find it painful to watch them learn the hard way. Isn't this just like us with God? We may act like we know it all. We think we can handle things on our own, that we don't need to bother God with the matter, or we're tired of waiting on God to bring change.

In order to shut this open door, surrender your ways praying, *"Not my will, but Yours be done"* (Luke 22:42b NIV). Recognize that God's power is made perfect in your weaknesses (2 Corinthians 12:9 NIV), not in your strengths. Life is uncertain. Things can change in an instant. Whether you're on the mountaintop or in the valley, put your confidence in the Lord and claim the promises of these verses in Jeremiah, *"Blessed is the one who trusts in the LORD, whose confidence is in Him. They will be like a tree planted by the water that sends out its roots by the stream. It does not fear when heat comes; its leaves are always green. It has no worries in a year of drought and never fails to bear fruit"* (Jeremiah 17:7-8 NIV). What wonderful promises to stand on!

Beware comparing yourself to others. When we compare ourselves to others, it results in one of two outcomes: either we win the comparison game and feel that we are better than, or we lose and feel less than. We work hard to create an outward façade that puts us in the winner's circle of the comparison game, but that is not where God calls us to put our time, energy, or resources.

Take the hypocritical Pharisees for example. Jesus warned the crowds to *"beware the teachers of the religious law. For they parade around in flowing robes and receive respectful greetings…and pretend to be pious by making long prayers in public"* (Mark 12:38-40 NLT). How sad that the men who were supposed to be the most godly were trapped in a "holier than thou" comparison game. Their spiritual pride blinded them from seeing Jesus as the Redeemer from the Old Testament prophecies, causing them to persecute Him as a blasphemer instead.

Social media is a modern-day example of a platform where we can airbrush our lives and our bodies to make them appear better than they really are. Façades fashioned by our own hands to win the comparison game. We place great importance on the externals, but God focuses on the internal. As we studied before, when God was looking for a new king, He told Samuel, *"Do not consider his appearance or his height…the LORD does not look at the things people look at. People look at the outward appearance, but the LORD looks at the heart"* (1 Samuel 16:7 NIV). Spending your time, energy, and resources on cultivating the soil of your heart to be more like Jesus instead of your social media platform closes the door to pride.

Beware glorifying yourself over God. When you receive praise for the outstanding job you are doing at work, for what the wonderful event you planned, for the delicious meal you prepared, for the excellent speech you gave…you have to admit, it feels pretty good. However, when we pridefully bask in the limelight of our success, we step into the spotlight of God's glory. It is easy to gravitate towards immediate recognition and lose sight of the eternal rewards awaiting us. Let us not forget that God did not create us to bring ourselves glory; He created us for His glory (Isaiah 43:7 NIV).

God desires to be glorified not just in our success but also in our weakness. Because pride includes insecurity, we are inclined to hide our perceived weaknesses, failures, and mistakes. When we do this, we rob God of the opportunity to be glorified in our weaknesses. Let me explain. 2 Corinthians 4:6-8 says, *"For God, who said, 'Let there be light in the darkness,' has made his light shine in our hearts…but we are like fragile clay jars containing this treasure. This makes it clear that our great power is from God, not from ourselves"* (NLT). Here, the apostle Paul describes us as earthen vessels, jars of clay, that house the treasure of His light and His power in our hearts. If we desire to let God's light radiate in our lives, how is His light supposed to shine through us if we cover all the broken places of our earthen vessel? If we let God shine through us both in our successes and in our failures, then we can close the door to pride by allowing God to be glorified through us.

Engage with God

o   What open doors did God reveal to you that need to be closed to prevent pride from creeping in?

o   What practical strategies can you implement to change your attitudes and actions?

Enabled through Spiritual Practice

Pride can blind us to seeing areas in our lives that are in need of change. The practice of self-examination opens our hearts to God and invites Him to show us areas that need attention. This is a difficult exercise because we don't like to see our sin or focus on our weaknesses. As you prayerfully consider areas that God is asking you to change, remember, God exposes the truth so that *"the truth will set you free"* (John 8:32 NIV). With that in mind, try this exercise.

o   Ask God to reveal an area of pride you need to work on
o   When God reveals that area, start by thanking Him for bringing it to light
o   Then confess your pride to Him
o   Using palms down, palms up, release that area to God and open your hands to receive what God has for you to replace the area you gave over to Him
o   Ask God to show you any changes you can make to keep that prideful area from returning
o   Ask God to transform this prideful area for His glory
o   Record what you learn

Day 3
Enlightened through Scripture Study

Pray

Lord, I confess all the ways that I think about myself more than I think about You. Help me to keep my thoughts fixed on You (Isaiah 26:3 NLT). Remove the prideful areas of my heart. Teach me how to surrender those areas to You in a spirit of humility. Help the desire of my heart to truly be, not my will but Yours be done. In Jesus' name I pray, amen.

Observe

Passage: 1 Peter 5:5-7 (NASB)

Since this is a shorter passage, it would be helpful to read the surrounding verses in order to understand the context in which these verses were written.

Word studies can often give us new insight into a passage by helping us look at the Hebrew or Greek meaning of the word. Since this passage is found in the New Testament, written in Greek, we will be looking at Greek roots.

- o   As you begin observing the passage, mark all references to the word *humility* in the same way.
- o   Then, look up the Greek words for humble, humility, and proud. Note the Greek word, its definition, and its grammatical form (noun, verb, adverb, etc.) then reread the passage with that definition in mind. Record any new insights you have.
- o   In this passage, Peter gives a warning about prideful people. What do you think Peter is saying about pride? About humility?

Interpret

At the end of verse 5, there is a quote referencing another passage of Scripture (in some translations this will appear all in capital letters). The small letter next to the words quoted signals the reader where else these words appear in Scripture. Using a concordance (noted in the margin of your Bible or online), you can look up the other passages for help to discern more clearly what the passage being studied is saying. This is called cross-referencing.

- o   Look up these verses and record what you learn.
- o   Record where you found them and what you learn about pride and humility.
    - o   James 4:6, 10
    - o   Proverbs 3:34
    - o   Luke 18:14
    - o   Proverbs 29:23
    - o   Proverbs 16:18
    - o   Genesis 3:1-6

Apply/Engage with God

o How did the Scripture study change your view of pride and humility?

o What does it mean for you to clothe yourself in humility to others?

o In what areas do you need to humble yourself under the mighty hand of God?

Enabled through Spiritual Practice

When we personalize Scripture by inserting our own name or the name of another, we avail ourselves to God's magnificent power to change our lives. Once you have released those areas you've been holding tightly to, practice claiming God's promises for yourself as you insert your name into the passages below:

o **Isaiah 41:10** – *"So do not fear, _____, for I am with you; do not be dismayed, for I am your God. I will strengthen you and help you; I will uphold you with my righteous right hand."*

o **Psalm 27:14** – *"Wait for the Lord, _____; be strong and take heart and wait for the Lord."*

o **Psalm 145:18-19** – *"The Lord is near to _____, who calls on him, to all who call on him in truth. He fulfills the desires of those who fear him; he hears their cry and saves them."*

o **Philippians 4:6-7** – *"Do not be anxious about anything, _____, but in every situation, by prayer and petition, with thanksgiving, present your requests to God. And the peace of God, which transcends all understanding, will guard your hearts and your minds in Christ Jesus."*

Day 4
Encouraged: Sara's Story

No one ever wants to be known as prideful. It's not something one strives for nor is it something to be desired, yet here I was, sitting there internally convicted that I had become a very prideful person. You also don't just become prideful overnight. There are small things that if let go unnoticed manifest into pride, and that is where I was.

I had issues. At age eight, a neighbor was charged with sexually abusing me, along with two other girls while babysitting us. Though it began with just him, he was soon joined with his eldest son, and by the time I was 9 years old, men were coming over to pay for time with me. At 10 years old, while the son raped me, I decided it was time to fight back. Due to this, I was hit on the head and left alone in the woods. Thankfully, I was discovered and the abuse finally stopped.

After the abuse had stopped, I thought everything else in my life would improve as well. However, I soon realized that a deep-rooted disgust with myself had continued to grow. Due to this, it became common to be mistreated and bullied at school. I was often called "fat" and "ugly," though looking back, I was not at all fat nor ugly. I could not understand why they were so mean to me, so I began to eat less and exercise more. This change in behavior brought compliments, making me want to continue what I was doing. I was finally feeling accepted.

As a freshman in high school, I made the varsity cheerleading squad. The team was not happy to have a freshman on board, so one day they put me against a locker and circled the areas on my body they felt were too fat. I wanted so bad to feel accepted that I took what they said to heart. I stopped eating almost completely, and in 10th grade, I ended up in a psychiatric ward.

This is where the battle for control began. As the ward staff force-fed me, making sure I got enough calories, I responded with bulimia. I had the control to vomit all they made me eat. After leaving the hospital, I also began experimenting with diet pills, which gave me more feelings of control. This cycle continued until I was a sophomore in college. By then I had been engaging in eating disordered behaviors for so long, I didn't know how to stop. I felt trapped and bound tightly by this eating disorder. When I finally reached out for help, I spent the next year of my life in and out of psych hospitals, IOP, partial programs, and intensive therapy where the "help" that I was receiving simply felt like another form of bullying. I was told that I would never recover and that eventually, I would die from an eating disorder. There was no hope, no peace, and I would never again be "normal." So, I gave up.

I blamed everything outside of me for my eating disorder. It was because of the abuse as a child and from being bullied at school. I was convinced that no one wanted me or could help me. I continued in this cycle of belief until a Bible study challenged me to look at things differently. As I began to look inward, I discovered that the issue was not how others treated me, but how I reacted. The deepest root was pride. It was hard for me to accept, but I followed it through and found it was an issue in me that blocked success for me in many areas. My eating disorder constantly had me desiring control. This meant that I put God on the backburner. As we learned in the lesson, pride can include comparisons, manipulation, selfishness, impatience, perfectionism, competition, defensiveness, and judgment…all of which the eating disorder used to fuel its nasty fire within me.

As I moved on to learn how to be transformed and get rid of my pride issue, I learned more and had to go deeper with God. I found out that the opposite of pride is humility. I learned that humility is thinking of yourself less and thinking of who God, and what He has for your life, more. Thinking I was a humble person, this cut deeply because I was far from this. Daily, I am sure I thought more about myself than the average human. I was constantly obsessing over how much I ate, how I looked, how my clothes fit me, how much weight I could lose, etc. that I had completely and utterly become obsessed over ME. That is literally the most prideful and least humble statement one could ever make, and it was coming out of my mouth!

Even though I am a broken person, I have hope because of God. I developed an eating disorder at 15. I am 28 years old now, which means that I have battled with an eating disorder for half of my life. This issue of pride was so deeply rooted and so intricately entangled into every aspect of my life that I had not realized that it was there. I was so focused on the eating disorder and me, which turned into cyclical chaos in my life. When I learned to keep my eyes on Jesus, things changed. Knowing God walks with me and really cares about me helps me survive the daily lies in my mind so that I can hear the truth. I gained more control and happiness in my life than I ever had before. Surrendering brings more freedom than one can imagine. Whereas pride leads to shame and secrets, humility leads to a life filled with adventure and growth. As I continue to break the chains of pride in my life, I also continue to break the chains of the eating disorder that had taken so much from me. I am getting stronger because of God, and I know that one day, I will be completely free from the eating disorder.

Engage with God

o   What about Sara's story resonated with you?

o   Pride kept Sara from moving forward in her recovery. How is pride keeping you stuck in your own eating and body image struggles?

Enabled through Spiritual Practice

Consider this illustration used by author, Leslie Vernick.[3] Imagine drawing a tree. At the bottom of the trunk draw a heart and at the top of the trunk draw some branches. On the branches write some manifestations of pride like comparisons, bitterness, perfectionism, discontentment, and the like. A person can work hard to remove the characteristics described on each branch from their lives but without addressing the root problem of pride, new branches or new manifestations will grow in their place because the heart hasn't changed.

Think about that for a minute. As this truth sinks in, be gentle with yourself. Don't let your mind go to condemnation, shame, worthlessness, hopelessness, or despair. *"There is no condemnation for those who belong to Christ Jesus"* (Romans 8:1-2 NLT). Remember, God doesn't reveal our sin to condemn us but to transform us. When we allow God to change our hearts, our root systems and then our branches will no longer bear prideful behaviors. Instead, we will bear fruit from a changed heart, which are *"love, joy, peace, patience, kindness, goodness, faithfulness, gentleness, and self-control"* (Galatians 5:22-23 NASB).

As Christians, we are recognized by our fruit (Matthew 7:16 ESV). Take some time to take inventory of the fruit you are bearing. What is it rooted in—pride or humility? How would you be recognized by the fruit you are bearing? Ask God to reveal any changes you need to make and record what you hear. Then use palms down, palms up to tangibly release those things to Him.

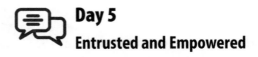

Day 5
Entrusted and Empowered

The lens of our worldview causes us to equate humility with weakness, low self-esteem, and passivity. On the contrary, biblical humility doesn't render us powerless; rather it empowers us to carry out the kingdom work God has planned for you. 1 Peter 5:5-7 shows us that humility requires submission of our will to God. As we bow low in God's presence, He promises to give us grace and exalt us in His own way and timing. Therefore, humility means willingly accepting the task assigned to you by your heavenly Father, regardless of how it appears, and trusting that in His infinite wisdom, He has chosen what is best for you. (For more insight, read Luke 14:7-11.)

Hannah Hurnard, in her allegory *Hinds' Feet on High Places*,[4] beautifully illustrates this process of surrender to God and the transformation it brings as the reader accompanies a crippled, disfigured main character named Much-Afraid on her pilgrimage to the High Places of victory and union with Christ. The author describes in the preface the premise behind Much-Afraid's storyline of how believers glean life-changing lessons on their faith journeys:

> *"The only way is by learning to accept, day by day, the actual conditions and tests permitted by God, by a continually repeated laying down of our own will and acceptance of his as it is presented to us… every acceptance of his will becomes an altar of sacrifice and every such surrender and abandonment of ourselves to his will is a means of furthering us on the way to the High Places to which he desires to bring every child of his while they are still living on earth."*

God is inviting us on a journey with Him to the High Places. Friend, our God is a good God who has your best interests in mind. However, God may give you a difficult assignment. He may be asking you to love someone who is unlovable, to walk through the challenges of recovering from an eating disorder, to shepherd a difficult child. Even though you may not understand your assignment like Much-Afraid, put your hope and trust in Him. He is faithful to complete the good work He starts. *"For from Him and through Him and for Him are all things"* (Romans 11:36 NIV). Rest in the knowledge that God's will is better than your own regardless of the outcome. To be able to truly say, "Not my will but Yours be done"—that's humility.

It takes a humble spirit to acknowledge our need for God and to understand that God's *"power works best in weakness"* (2 Corinthians 12:9 NLT). God has given us power through Jesus' death on a cross to overcome the power of sin. *"And because you belong to Him, the power of the life-giving Spirit has freed you from the power of sin that leads to death"* (Romans 8:1-2 NIV). What good news! We can transform our pride by walking in a spirit of humility.

Engage with God

o   Is there a difficult assignment that God has asked you to undertake?

o   What will it look like for you to clothe yourself in humility as you carry out this assignment?

Enabled through Spiritual Practice

We have been practicing releasing anything we grasp onto tightly over to God. I encourage you to take it one step further by confiding in a friend or loved one. Sharing our struggles with others can be difficult because often we are too proud to let others know we are hurting and because it feels like we're admitting failure. However, if we shift how we view failure and separate our view of ourselves from the sin, it changes everything. Author Leslie Vernick reframes failure by saying, "Failure is not a statement about you. It's a statement about what happened."[5] Choosing to accept our mistakes and learn from them, instead of letting them define us, breaks down prideful barriers and makes it easier to ask for help when we need it.

Separating yourself from the sin is the first step and confessing it to someone else is the second. Confession is important for several reasons: First, sin thrives in secrecy. Confession brings what was hidden in darkness into the light and change can begin. No one can change what they can't see. Second, when we *"confess [our] sins to each other,"* we allow the body of Christ to *"pray for each other so that [we] may be healed"* (James 5:16). Then, third, when we pray, Jesus promises that *"where two or three gather together as my followers, I am there among them"* (Matthew 18:20 NLT). Is there someone you trust and with whom you can confess and pray in regards to an area where you need God's grace and strength in overcoming? I challenge you to reach out and share your struggles with them. Consider using Scripture when you pray like we practiced earlier in the week.

ENDNOTES

1   Jim Samra, Article: "Pride and Humility" (Grand Rapids, MI, 2013).
2   Rick Warren, *The Purpose Driven Life* (Grand Rapids, MI: Zondervan, 2002), Day 19.
3   Leslie Vernick, Available online at *leslievernick.com*. 13 October 2016.
4   Hannah Hurnard, *Hinds' Feet on High Places* (Wheaton, IL: Tyndale House, 1975), ix.
5   Leslie Vernick, Available online at *leslievernick.com*. "Empowered to Change," 23 April, 2019.

Session 9
Transformed: From Legalistic to Grace Filled

Day 1
Enlisted to Expose the Darkness

I remember the day when my oldest learned to ride a bike. He had been riding confidently with his training wheels for some time. One summer morning, my husband awakened with the idea that today was the day to take the training wheels off. My son waited excitedly while my husband removed the worn wheels from each side. Once he finished, my son enthusiastically got on his bike with a look of determination and expectation. However, the second my husband let go of the seat and he began to wobble, a look of panic swept over him. In an instant he realized he no longer had his training wheels to rely on to hold him steady, and the confidence he once had was now gone. He called out in an alarming shrill, "Dad!" His dad was right there, jogging next to him and quickly grabbed the back of the seat to keep him from falling. And so it went for the next few laps around the cul-de-sac. I saw my son's confidence grow with each lap as he trusted his dad to help him and no longer had to rely on his training wheels for stability.

Isn't this a picture of us? We are constantly looking to other things to hold us steady when the reality is our heavenly Father is right there, jogging alongside of us. Sometimes rules, intended to help just like training wheels, become our stabilizing force instead of God. In fact, anything that acts as a false sense of security can mask itself as training wheels in your life. What foolishness panic and fear can bring out in us. Often our first response is to turn to earthly things to cope instead of turning to God for rescue. However, I know from personal experience that those things instead pull us down into a cycle of destruction and despair. Friend, when you start to wobble, remember God's jogging alongside you and readily waiting for you to ask Him for help.

Engage with God

o   What are some of the things you turn to for rescue, and what are the results of those choices?

o   What training wheels exist in your life, and are you trusting in them more than God to rescue you?

Enabled through Spiritual Practice

You already learned how to apply the discipline of meditation and have been practicing the discipline of Scripture study in each session. This week, we will focus on pairing the two together, because meditation on Scripture and Scripture study are fundamental components of our spiritual walk.

Scripture study is important because *"all Scripture is God-breathed and is useful for teaching, rebuking, correcting and training in righteousness so that the servant of God may be thoroughly equipped for every good work"* (2 Timothy 3:16-17). That means that spending time in Scripture is a primary avenue that God can use to teach and train us in His way. Also, God promises that His Word will *"always produces fruit...accomplish all [He] wants it to and...prosper everywhere [He] sends it"* (Isaiah 55:11 NLT).

The Scripture study section in Day 3 has three different passages to work through. so plan accordingly. As you spend extra time in the Word this week, I pray that God would do a transformative work in your heart and your mind.

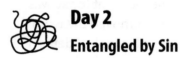

Day 2
Entangled by Sin

From a young age, I was a rule follower. I learned quickly that things went better for me when I obeyed. My obedience brought words of praise, warm smiles, and reassuring hugs for my efforts. When I became a Christian, I desired to obey God's law and worked diligently to follow it like any good rule follower would. Soon, however, I became rule-focused instead of God-focused, and I developed a false sense of security in them. In essence, I had shifted from obedience to legalism.

In order to understand the shift, let's unpack God's law and legalism. All throughout the Old Testament, we see God giving His people instructions for upright living. God created these guidelines for their good, for their protection, and He desired their obedience to Him to flow out of their love for Him. Therefore, as followers of God, we are called to obey His commands, and He takes delight in our obedience. Legalism, on the other hand, is defined as "dependence on moral law rather than religious faith." Israel tried *"to get right with God by keeping the law, not by trusting in Him"* (Romans 9:32 NLT). Furthermore, when God sent His Son into the world, it wasn't to abolish the Law but to fulfill it (Matthew 5:17). However, to legalists like the Pharisees, that is exactly what it felt like. They had strictly adhered to every law God had given thus far and took pride in their ability to follow it as if somehow they were holier for doing it. Then when Jesus arrived on the scene claiming to be the Messiah, He healed on the Sabbath and socialized with unclean people. They could not accept Him. They had placed legalism (their strict adherence to the law) on the throne of their hearts instead of God, offering them what every idol offers—nothing. They couldn't see how Jesus was the fulfillment of the Scriptures they held dear since rule following was only for outward display, not an inward demonstration of their hearts.

The intent of the law was never to put it before God. Remember that anything we put before God is an idol. And so it was for me. I unwittingly allowed the law to become the object of my worship instead of God. That is exactly how I went awry. I had noble intentions in my desire to obey God's Law, but slowly I began trusting in the rules more than I trusted in God. Rules gave me a sense of stability when things weren't stable, a plan to follow when there wasn't a plan. This framework fell apart when my world went into a tailspin, and the training wheels no longer offered me any stability. You see, in my struggle with an eating disorder, my rules dictated my life. They became a way for me to determine how I did that day, whether something was good or bad, or if I was good or bad.

I discovered the harm in this way of thinking when I started intensive eating disorder treatment. I was fortunate to have a treatment team comprised of renowned experts in the field. I followed their directives, reluctantly but obediently, and I made great strides emotionally and physically under their expert care. I did this hoping that this plan was the "magic formula" that would rescue me and remove every last trace of the eating disorder from my life. However, I was essentially replacing an unhealthy set of rules with a healthy set of rules, but still trusting in the rules and in others for rescue instead of God.

Paul describes this situation well in his letter to the Colossians:

> *"Since you died with Christ to the elemental spiritual forces of this world, why, as though you still belonged to the world, do you submit to its rules? These rules…are based on merely human commands and teachings. Such regulations indeed have an appearance of wisdom; with their self-imposed worship, their false humility and their harsh treatment of the body, but they lack any value in restraining sensual indulgence"* (Colossians 2:20-23 NIV).

Reading these verses was an eye-opening moment. My self-imposed rules weren't based on truth but worldly desires and human created ideals (many of which were my own). They seemed to offer wisdom, the answers I was looking for, but instead they caused great harm to my body, to my personhood, and to my soul. They betrayed me, and there was no formula, no recipe for success. I realize now that I was essentially taking God out of the process and looking to my ability to rescue myself instead of His. Likewise, my results weren't freedom, rather they were captivity and idolatry. It was a works-based methodology that left me constantly striving yet condemned for not meeting its insatiable standards. I needed a remedy. I needed grace.

> *Grace: the free and unmerited favor of God*[1]

Ephesians 2:8 says, *"For it is by grace you have been saved, through faith—and this is not from yourselves, it is the gift of God"* (NIV). A gift from God for me? Yes, and for you too. Unmerited grace by definition is given to one who doesn't deserve it. Maybe you think you've fallen too far for God to save you, that you are a continuous failure, that you'll never measure up. So, you cling to legalism, rigid rules, to somehow purify yourself or feel assurance that you're "good."

> *D. L. Moody says it this way, "The Law tells me how crooked I am. Grace comes along and straightens me out."*

This is where I went wrong. I thought following the rules would straighten me out, but that left no room for God's grace to do its transformative work. No matter what you have done, God purified you and declared you free of sin when Jesus paid for your sin and mine on the cross (Romans 3:24). Your salvation is a free gift. All you have to do is accept it.

Maybe we can agree that salvation is a free gift, but you feel you don't deserve it. If you view God as legalistic, then it is logical that you would view yourself in the same way—defining your self-worth by your own ability to follow God's commands. But legalism causes us to live in the black and white, in absolutes, and that is not how life works. Life is full of gray areas that don't fit into the black or the white categories, and that often produces anxiety. While God's law is perfect, pure, and righteous, the law alone cannot and will not save you. Only by the grace of God through the shed blood of Jesus Christ on the cross are you saved.

Friend, God loves you regardless of what you've done in the past, what you did today, or what you will do tomorrow. Legalism compels by giving us the illusion of control, order, symmetry, something by which to evaluate our performance. Grace seems scary because it doesn't give a measure, just love. It forces us to accept our imperfections, taking them out of our hands, and placing them into God's hands—putting God in control, not us. That feels like a scary place to me. Maybe it does to you too?

The truth is we cannot transform ourselves, our life, or our situations through legalism. Take this opportunity to confess to God any way you've clung to rules more than Him. Join me in relinquishing fears of letting go, resting, and trusting in the knowledge that what God has in store for us is better than whatever we can come up with on our own. It's time to stop trusting in the training wheels and start riding our bikes in faith. Take comfort. God won't let you fall. He's always right there jogging next to you.

Engage with God

o   In what ways do you struggle with legalism?

o   How do you react to yourself or others when your "rules" aren't followed, and how would you react differently if you were walking in the mindset of grace?

o   Do you find it harder to extend grace to others or to yourself, and does that stand in your way to see yourself or others as God does?

Enabled through Spiritual Practice

Practicing meditation can guard your heart from the world and "submitting to its rules" as Paul outlined in his letter to the Colossians. If these rules and regulations are the focus of your thoughts, how can you expect to change? Proverbs 4:23 says, *"Above all else, guard your heart for everything you do flows from it"* (NIV). Meditation on Scripture keeps God's Word at the forefront of our minds so that what flows from our hearts reflects God, not the world. Likewise, when we meditate on the truths we have learned through Scripture study, it brings depth to those truths and cements them in our hearts, further establishing and strengthening our foundation. This practice opens the door for transformation.

Let's practice it together. First, write a list of the different rules and regulations that dictate your life on a piece of scrap paper. Next read the list out loud. Once you have done that, declare that you refuse to "belong to the world" or "submit to its rules" anymore. Then shred your paper in a paper shredder or by hand to acknowledge that you will no longer live this way.

Now that your mind has been cleared, begin meditating on the verses below taken from the text above. Allow God the space to speak, rebuke, direct, and transform you from the inside out as you slowly and contemplatively contemplate each word.

- o **Matthew 5:17b** – *"Do not think that I (Jesus) came to abolish the Law…I did not come to abolish but to fulfill"* (NASB).
- o **Colossians 2:20-23** – *"Since you died with Christ to the elemental spiritual forces of this world, why, as though you still belonged to the world, do you submit to its rules?…These rules…are based on merely human commands and teachings. Such regulations indeed have an appearance of wisdom, with their self-imposed worship, their false humility and their harsh treatment of the body, but they lack any value in restraining sensual indulgence"* (NIV).
- o **Ephesians 2:8-9** – *"For it is by grace you have been saved, through faith—and this is not from your- selves, it is the gift of God—not by works so that no one can boast"* (NIV).
- o **Romans 3:23-24** – *"For all have sinned and fall short of the glory of God, and all are justified freely by His grace through the redemption that came by Christ Jesus"* (NIV).

Day 3
Enlightened and Enabled through Scripture Study

Today, you will be practicing the discipline of Scripture study by doing a more extensive study of three different passages on the topic of legalism and grace. As always, record any verses that stand out to you and why. May the Lord bless you as you dig into His Word.

At the end of this section, take the time to reflect on the in-depth study of Scripture you completed for the week. If in a group, share with each other what God revealed to each one of you individually and celebrate it. It may be something different for everyone because our God speaks directly and personally to each one of us!

Pray

Forgive me, Lord, for all the ways I have looked to external methods and relied on my own self-will to res- cue me. Help me to receive mercy and find grace from You to help me in my time of need (Hebrews 4:16). Thank You, Lord, that no matter how many times I make mistakes, Your grace still finds me and covers me. In Jesus' name I pray, amen.

Observe

Passage 1: Ephesians 2:4-10 (NASB)

Every word in Scripture is God-breathed and has been chosen for a purpose. Further investigation of the meaning of the words employed can bring new understanding.

- o Look up the definition of the word *grace* and record what you learn.
- o Mark the word *grace* in the passage in the same way each time it appears.
- o Make a list of what you learn about grace from the passage.

Interpret

- o Look back at the definition of the word *grace*. In your own words, write a brief definition of grace as if you were sharing this concept with a young child.
- o Refer back to your list on grace. Record what you learn about God and His love for us.
- o Take note of the words *so that* in verses 7 and 9. Paul uses those words to give us the reason why God did things that way. What did you learn?

Apply/Engage with God

What great love God has for us! Ask God if there is anything that makes it hard for you to receive God's love and grace and then give it over to Him to transform.

- o How will you show grace and love differently to others and to yourself as a result of what you learned?

- o Ask God what next step you could take to implement what you learned.

Passage 2: Luke 13:10-17 (NIV)

Observe

It is important to identify the different characters in the passage. First and foremost, look for and mark *God the Father*, *Jesus*, and *Holy Spirit* in the passage.

- o There are four characters in this story: the woman, the religious leaders, the people and Jesus. Make a list with four columns recording what you learn about what each character says and does.
- o Observe the conflict happening in this passage. Whom is it between and why?
- o Mark the key word *Sabbath* in the same way throughout the passage. Record what you learn.

Interpret

- o Why is there such great conflict between Jesus and the synagogue leaders? What is the bigger issue here that is causing the uproar?
- o Use a Bible dictionary or commentary to learn more about the importance of the Sabbath in Jewish culture. What was the Jewish law regarding the Sabbath? Why were the religious leaders so upset by this?

o   What is your view of the Sabbath and the role it should play in our lives today?

Apply/Engage with God

o   Look back over your list of the four different characters in the story. What character do you relate to the most? Why? If you were that person, write about your experience from their point of view, think about what you would think and feel about Jesus, and contemplate what action you might take.

o   Are you allowing religious rules to be an obstacle in your relationship with God? If so, how and what might you do to change that?

Passage 3: Matthew 5:17-44 (NASB)

Observe and Interpret

Contrasts help us to compare two things that are different from one another and are easily spotted surrounding the word *but*. Let's practice together. Notice these contrasts and record what you learn.

o   Note the beginning words of verses 21, 27, 31, 33, 38, and 43. Does this imply fact or rumor and why?

o   Note the beginning words of verses 22, 28, 32, 34, 39, and 44. Observe who is speaking and how this differs from what you just observed in the last question.

The tool of cross-referencing helps to bring greater meaning and understanding to the text by comparing Scripture with Scripture. In verse 43, it says, *"You have heard that is was said, 'YOU SHALL LOVE YOUR NEIGHBOR and hate your enemy.'"* Notice the phrase in capital letters.* This indicates that another section of Scripture is being quoted. Underline each phrase in capital letters (or in quotes if using a different translation) and look up the corresponding cross reference.**

Now, notice how the first half of verse 43 is in caps and the second half isn't. That tells us that the first section is quoting Scripture, but the second half is not. Take note of how they added their own laws to God's Law.

o   Make three columns. On the left, record the sections that quote other parts of Scripture. In the middle, record what the Pharisees added. On the right, record what Jesus says about it.
o   Take note of how the Pharisees were focused on outward demonstration, but God looks at inward motivation.

Note: Reading the passage in the NASB translation makes the contrasts easier to identify since all Scripture references are printed in capital letters.

**Using a concordance either online or in your Bible, use the subscript letters next to the phrase to help you locate the corresponding cross reference. For more a more detailed explanation of inductive study, see the Appendix.*

Apply/Engage with God

o   Are you more caught up in outward demonstration or inward motivation? Make a list of at least five rules you live by and then ask God to help you uncover your motives behind them. Who are you trying to please by keeping them, God or man?

o   We studied about Eve in the Garden of Eden and saw how Satan subtly changes the truth and then in turn we make it part of our law. Don't we do the same thing? Refer back to the list of rules and regulations you made in the reflection section. Ask God to reveal to you any partial truths that may be misleading you, reflect on how those half-truths were shaped, and replace them with truth.

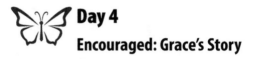

Day 4
Encouraged: Grace's Story

"You're just not pushing enough, Grace." The coach sat behind his desk like a judge in a courtroom.

I agreed…I had to do more. Field and track were so important to me. If I worked out more and ate less, my performance should increase. This thinking pattern triggered my need to control all situations and made me feel that everything in my life was not good enough. I had to do more to be acceptable.

As I started losing weight, I felt so proud and couldn't get enough of the excitement of another pound dropping off. I wanted more, for I never felt thin enough. It was my focus and nothing else mattered. I struggled for years with anorexia and excessive exercising, and it almost took my life.

I became bulimic and ate as I wanted only to purge it out. This lasted for several years, and over a 17-year period, I bounced back and forth repeatedly in this vicious cycle. Some years, I was aware of the eating disorder but didn't feel like I needed help, even though it controlled much of my life. At other times, it was loud and cruel, and I suffered every waking moment, which would lead me back into treatment. Over the last year, I have taken steps to have a closer relationship with God. I want to destroy this eating disorder, and I know with God's help, it will happen. God's plan for me is more than I can imagine. He wants to break the chains of this eating prison and free me. His gifts are there for me, but I have not used them. As I become free, I will be able to use them to their full capacity and worship and praise Him fully…and live for Him alone.

Working through the mangled emotions and feelings I carry has been difficult. I'm so angry and I keep it inside. Processing it is healthier. I know that, so why don't I do it? Suffering gets me depressed. From my past, horrible memories submerge my being, and I can't seem to get through them. There is a wall that keeps me from moving forward. The cement in the wall is fear. I fear everything. Control cannot be found, and I want it so desperately.

Fear makes me feel so lonely. There is so much pain…the attacks…the disappointment. What is the way of escape? I can't find it, so the low self-esteem I feel creates an identity for my eating disorder. I become my disorder.

What can I control? My need for approval and perfection places a mask on my face. I don't want to lie to people about how I am doing, but I can't seem to reveal the real me that makes others uncomfortable. Who I am is not acceptable and I should be hidden away.

The culture demands that I act in a certain way. I cannot do it. I am not a part of my culture but an outsider. My family was not acceptable, so it only makes sense that I would not be either. We're weird. We don't fit the mold. We're different.

ED felt like my one and only true friend. It comforted me when life was painful. Nothing else helped me like ED. I believed I could trust it and control it. Without this friend I would be lost. Life would be horrible without its presence. It was me. Nothing the counselors, dietitians, parents, friends, or even God would tell me did I believe. These lies led me into depression, and I couldn't move on. I don't like conflict and avoid situations like the plague. I use ED during these times. I know God should be the one I turn to, but I want instant gratification. ED gives me that while God sometimes takes time to work. Although God's process lasts a lot longer, it takes more time the traditional way. Of course, afterwards there is always guilt knowing what I should do. It's a band-aid. It's not long before the pain returns.

My relationship with God became more intimate as I dove deeper into His Word. It's the key and is activated only with truly believing Him and His Word. On-fire seasons of strong faith cause me to see God's miracles. I can see how useless the ED is and that I don't really need it in my life.

Doubt seasons always seem to creep into my life…I'm not sure about God and life. The ED becomes my go-to instead of God. With the night and day difference, I should be able to stay in the spot where the chaos dissolves, but I don't always. My faith is weak, and I need to cry out, "Lord, I believe, help my unbelief!"

My flesh strongly believes that the ED is the cure of my problems. How could I believe that? It's hard to ask God for help when I fly to ED because it's so easy. Proverbs 14:12 says, *"There is a way that seems right to a man, but its end is the way of death."* That's my truth. Controlling my ED is my goal. I will die if I don't. What's it like to have a life without ED? I don't know. I do know that it always leads to a dead end. I have lost so much in life because of it, including relationships, jobs, etc. No good comes from it. It always looks promising when I am in its midst, but ED never delivers.

My mind controls most of what I do. My life revolves around ED and consumes me. I must focus on what is truth versus lies to break from the addiction. Romans 12:2 says, *"Do not be conformed to the pattern of this world, but be transformed by the renewing of your mind. Then you will be able to test and approve what God's will is…his good, pleasing and perfect will."*

Another truth to remember is John 10:10. "The thief's purpose is to steal and kill and destroy. My purpose is to give them a rich and satisfying life." This is God's truth. The lie says that you are not good enough.

False messages say you are a failure and will never get better. Protect your mind with the truth. The lie that you are beautiful only if you are thin…false. God tells us that our beauty comes from the inside. Proverbs 31:30 says, *"Charm is deceptive and beauty is fleeting, but a woman who fears the Lord will be praised."* I want to live my life with a sense of urgency. The distractions of the world are just not important. They are things that will fade away and not have eternal value.

Without God, there is no chance for me to succeed. Hope would be gone. With God, total freedom from food and weight obsession is mine. I press on to that truth and will make it.

Engage with God

o   How does legalism contribute to your eating and body image struggles?

o   How does pride and perfection play a role in legalism?

o   What parts of Grace's story resonated with you and what will you do as a result?

Enabled through Spiritual Practice

As you continue to meditate on the Scripture passages you've been studying this week, have any words or phrases impacted you? If not, ask God to give you a specific word to focus on. Let that word be the focus of your meditation today. Ask God what He might want to reveal to you through that word and how it applies to you personally. If you want to take it one step further, ask God to give you a word for the month or even for the year to meditate on. I practice this regularly and it is astounding to look back and see how that word gave me hope, direction, comfort, correction, or peace when God knew I would need it most.

Thank you for your diligence to dig into the Scriptures each and every week. God is pleased with your efforts to seek Him and spend time with Him. Your work is not in vain. God promises that His Word will always produce fruit and accomplish all He wants it to (Isaiah 55:11 NLT). So keep digging!

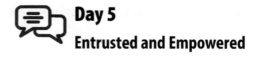 **Day 5**
Entrusted and Empowered

It is important to recognize that legalism, in the context of disordered eating, can be enslaving when both behavioral rituals and food selection dictate how you spend your time, energy, and resources. Just like food wasn't designed by God to be a stumbling block, rules weren't either. Author Judy Halliday, in her book *Thin Within*, sheds new light on this internal war between legalism and grace in the mind of a disordered eater and how grace is the remedy.

> *"In the case of those who struggle with disordered eating, the standard of legalism might be to be 'thin' to achieve a certain weight at all costs or the belief that when we 'lose weight' life will be perfect and we will be free from all our problems. When we adopt external methods to constrain our behavior we are buying the lie that victory can be won with our self-will. While 'losing weight' might result in an immediate increase in our sense of self-worth and value, it is temporary and does not change the deep-rooted feeling that we are irredeemably flawed nor does it satisfy our silent hunger for intimacy with God...striving for perfection, we are living the lie that we can make ourselves more acceptable to ourselves, to others and to God, if we just follow the letter of the law. Under grace we are free to turn to God as we really are, free to learn from our mistakes, free to change and grow and free to allow Him to help us to become all He intends us to be."[2]*

When we fall prey to the lie that following rules and regulations somehow makes us "more acceptable to ourselves, to others and to God, if we just follow the letter of the law," we become trapped in a works-based methodology that renders us powerless. Walking in grace removes the cloud of condemnation and empowers us with choices about what we turn to, what we rely on, and who sits on the throne of our hearts. Legalism is bondage. Grace is freedom. Friend, it's time to turn to grace. No turning back.

Engage with God

o   What rules and regulations have you made to make yourself "more acceptable to yourself, to others, and to God" if you just follow the letter of the law"?

o   What is God asking you to do to rely on Him and live free in His grace?

Enabled through Spiritual Practice

Taking time to stop and celebrate all the different markers in our lives is important. You most likely take time to celebrate birthdays and holidays, but do you take the time to celebrate your spiritual milestones? These can include how God has worked in your life, the ways that God has answered your prayers, and the trials that have brought you into a deeper relationship with Him. We must take time to remember God's many kindnesses to us (Psalm 106:7) because that helps us keep our eyes on Him. When we take our eyes off of God and forget what He's done is often when we stray and find the world more compelling and more appealing. Stop complaining about what you don't have and start celebrating what you do. Take some time to reflect on and celebrate the progress you've made over the course of this study and give God the glory for what He has done in your life.

If doing this in a group, start planning how you will celebrate upon completion of the study. Be creative, have fun, and give God the glory!

ENDNOTES

1 "grace," Merriam-Webster.com. 2011. Online, 15 May 2019.
2 Judy Halliday, R.N. and Arthur Halliday, M.D., *Thin Within: A Grace Oriented Approach to Lasting Weight Loss* (Nashville, TN: Thomas Nelson Publishers, 2005).

Transformed: From Ashamed to Honored

Day 1
Enlisted to Expose the Darkness

Well-known researcher Brené Brown has spent her life's work studying shame, vulnerability, and whole-heartedness. When describing the difference between shame and guilt, she says this:

> *"Shame is not the same as guilt. Guilt is feeling badly about breaking the vase. Shame is feeling that you are bad because you broke the vase. When we feel that we are bad, we don't feel that we are worthy of being loved."*[1]

Over the course of her research, Brown discovered that this pattern of turning to guilt or shame was often learned in childhood. The child either grows up believing they are inherently good, even when they make mistakes, or that they are inherently bad, regardless of the choices they make. God designed guilt to bring repentance, forgiveness, and freedom. When we feel accused, blamed, and belittled for our choices, the enemy sends shame to hold us captive, preventing God's light from shining in those dark places.

Friend, I don't know what your childhood was like. I don't know the things you have done, witnessed, endured, or overcome in your lifetime. I don't know if you feel worthy to be loved. But I do know this: as Ethel Waters would say, "God don't make no junk." You are not inherently bad; you are inherently good. You were designed and created by God. As we try and uncover together how shame is influencing you, impacting you, and ensnaring you, beware the enemy's attempts to pile on accusations and blame. Be gentle with yourself and let God cleanse, forgive, and replenish you anew as only He can.

Engage with God

Think about these questions with a pen in hand. Describe what areas of your past bring you the most shame. Are those areas the result of choices you made or from things done to you? What do you feel when you do something wrong now? Is guilt triggered bringing you to a place of repentance, or is shame triggered bringing you to a place brimming with failure and worthlessness? How do your past experiences shape how you respond when things go wrong?

As you journal, confess, repent, and release the areas of shame that are connected to your own poor choices, receive His grace and healing. If there are areas that bring you shame as a result of things that have been done to you or circumstances outside of your control, ask God if you are harboring any unforgiveness in your heart towards the other person, circumstance, or yourself. Record what you learn. (More on working through forgiveness in the next chapter.)

Enabled through Spiritual Practice

Scientific researchers estimate that the average American processes approximately 100,000 words a day. That's a lot of information flowing through our brains! Practicing the presence of God is a tool that can help keep us focused on Him and not let our thoughts get carried away by the rapid flow of information. In the beginning, it may help you to create prayers you can pray during specific events that occur in your everyday life. For example:

> While driving you might pray these words based on Psalm 139:5, 10, *"Lord, hem me in behind and before and lay Your hand upon me as I drive. Even there Your hand will guide me, Your right hand will hold me fast."*
>
> While showering you might pray these words based on Psalm 139:14, *"Lord, I praise You because I am fearfully and wonderfully made; Your works are wonderful, I know that full well. Help me to remember that about myself today."*
>
> While falling asleep you might pray these words based on Psalm 139:12, *"Thank You, Lord, that even the darkness will not be dark to You; the night will shine like the day, for darkness is as light to You."*
>
> You can also try it when you feel triggered by an emotion like shame. Try praying these words based on Psalm 25:2 and Psalm 84:11, *"Lord, help me to remember that those who trust in You will never be put to shame and that You Lord are the One who bestows favor and honor."*

Prayers like these can keep your thoughts centered on God throughout the day and turn your thoughts back to Him instead of getting swept away by your fleshy thoughts. Use the examples given or create your own and try practicing the presence of God this week.

Day 2
Entangled by Sin

Do you wear a badge of shame like Hester did in Nathaniel Hawthorne's literary classic *The Scarlet Letter*?[2] The main character, Hester, is publicly shamed for her adulterous act and forced by her Puritan society to wear an A for "adulterer" on her chest as a badge of humiliation, leaving her outwardly marked by her sin. Hester is forced to wrestle with questions about who she will let define her and if she can live in her community despite the ridicule.

Try to put yourself in her shoes. Think about what it would be like to have your sin on display for all to see, to be shunned and judged at first glance, to be defined by your community by your sinful acts. It would be devastating, demoralizing, crippling. I think we have all felt deep shame for something we have done or didn't do, that while we don't have anything branded on our chests, we still bear the weight of that sin like a boulder around our necks. When something like that weighs us down, it's hard to perform even the smallest everyday activities because the weight is so great. This doesn't allow us to flourish and live the abundant life God has for us. Instead of seeing light at the end of the tunnel, you see darkness. It's here in this dark place, where feelings of powerlessness and hopelessness cast large shadows over you and giving up becomes an alluring option.

I know this place. The "ED" (eating disorder) label I seemingly wore on my chest caused me to feel defined by my struggle, and it wasn't the kind of label I set out to have. My shame was rooted in the lie that because I struggled with an eating disorder, I had failed on every level. Failed my family, failed my friends, failed myself, but most of all, failed God. I berated myself, thinking that if only I had tried harder, then this would have been avoided altogether. Because I struggled to see myself as God sees me—fearfully and wonderfully made, His masterpiece, chosen, forgiven, redeemed, and loved by His everlasting love—I found myself stuck in a place of shame. Agreeing that those descriptors are true of myself was one thing, but believing it in my heart about myself was another. How incredibly hard it is to let God write His truth on our hearts especially when there are so many competing forces trying to write their own stories there as well.

While this concept of shame may not be new to you, inviting God to shine His light on your shame may be. Shame has plagued the lives of people for thousands of years, but a switch can be made when we invite God into the conversation. An example of this can be seen in Jesus' encounter with the woman at the well in the first half of John 4. In this story, John describes how Jesus crossed through Samaritan territory despite the fact that Jews regarded any contact with Samaritans to be defiling. Then Jesus decides to rest at the well and starts a conversation with a Samaritan woman who has come to draw water at mid-day by herself, despite the fact that Jewish men wouldn't speak to any woman alone. Jesus engages her in conversation and exposes the truth about her past failed relationships, her letter A if you will.

I can only imagine her face glowed hot with shame as her backstory was unveiled. Everyone else had excommunicated her. She had to go to the well at mid-day since she couldn't go with the other women at dawn or dusk. I picture her walking up to the well, seeing Jesus and bracing herself for judgment, condemnation, rebuke. But Jesus didn't respond like everyone else. He saw into her brokenness, recognized her unquenched heart, and responded with kindness. He surprises her with an offer of living water. Jesus says, *"Whoever drinks the water I give them will never thirst. Indeed, the water I give them will become in them a spring of water welling up to eternal life"* (John 4:14 NIV). She accepts His invitation and is immediately washed clean of her sin and shame. In this moment, her accusers are silenced, and God frees her from the shackles of her shame, transforming how both she and those around her perceive her. Her dignity restored, the woman walks away from the well with her head held high, leaving her life of scorn for a place of honor in God's kingdom.

Most of us fear having our sin exposed thinking it will lead to our demise, so we try desperately to hide it. Yet when we allow it to stay hidden, we allow our guilt to blossom into shame that weighs us down instead of causing us to turn from our sin. Max Lucado makes a point with the following quote:

> *"Not all guilt is bad. God uses appropriate doses of guilt to awaken us to sin. God's guilt brings enough regret to change us."*[3]

Jesus revealed the woman's sin not to condemn her but to set her free, and the same is true for us. When God reveals sin in our lives, we go quickly to condemnation, which brings shame, but *"God did not send His Son into the world to condemn the world, but to save the world through him"* (John 3:17 NIV). When God reveals sin in your life, don't condemn yourself. Instead, be gentle with yourself. Thank God that in His kindness He would root out the darkness in your heart instead of giving shame the opportunity to grow.

Jesus is offering you the same living water He offered the woman at the well. However, too often, we don't accept it because we feel unacceptable or too far gone to save. This lie readily ensnares us. Holly Gerth describes it well when she says,

> *"I think the enemy tricks us into believing we are not enough because he knows if we discover the truth, we'll be unstoppable."*[4]

It's time to stop shame-filled thinking and remember we are enough. Hebrews 12:2 tells us, *"We do this by keeping our eyes on Jesus, the champion who initiates and perfects our faith. Because of the joy awaiting him, he endured the cross, disregarding its shame"* (NLT). Jesus suffered the most humiliating and shameful death possible just so that you could experience new life with Him. Let that truth sink in.

He died for you.

The verse goes on to say, *"Now He is seated in the place of honor beside God's throne."* If Jesus is seated in the place of honor, what does that mean for you? It means that because Jesus took all our sin and shame with Him on the cross that day, those who accept Him become heirs, daughters of the King, royalty. We may be worthy of shame and undeserving of nobility, but Jesus' blood made us worthy of honor. Ask God to help you see yourself and your body as He sees it: worthy of honor.

Now that you know you are worthy of honor, start acting like it. First Corinthians 6:19-20 says, *"Don't you realize that your body is a temple of the Holy Spirit, who lives in you and was given to you by God? You do not belong to yourself, for God bought you with a high price. So, you must honor God with your body"* (NLT). Honor includes honoring ourselves and our bodies. Honor denotes respect, esteem, importance, appreciation, and value. I confess that many of my actions fail to demonstrate these beliefs about my body. What about you? If we don't treat ourselves and our bodies this way, how can we expect others to do so? Join me in making a pledge to daily start treating our bodies like a temple of the Holy Spirit and less like a discarded mistake. I know—easier said than done, but this change starts with you. This will require a change in our attitudes and our thinking. Second Corinthians 10:5 gives us instructions on how to do that, saying, *"We capture, like prisoners of war, every thought and insist that it bow in obedience to the Anointed One"* (TPT). Our job is to capture that thought and it's God's job to transform it. Now take Jesus' capable, reliable, and mighty hand that He is extending to you and walk with Him out of shame and into your rightful place of honor.

Engage with God

o   Ask the Lord what He might be asking you to do in order to transform your thinking about viewing yourself and your body as worthy of honor. Listen and record what you learn.

o   How do lies, fear, and pride play a role in keeping you stuck in shame?

Enabled through Spiritual Practice

Another way to practice the presence of God is by trying the method of fixed hour prayer, which means praying at a certain time of day. Believers praying at fixed hours of the day can be seen throughout Scripture, and this was adopted into practice by the early church, orthodox Jews, and monks. The set prayer schedule often gave structure to their days. It can do the same for us as well.

Since my schedule is often different every day, I set an alarm on my phone to remind me to stop and pray. If I wanted to pray some of the verses from this chapter, I might set my phone to alert me at 10:05 to remind me to pray 2 Corinthians 10:5, or at 12:02 to remind me to pray Hebrews 12:2, or at 6:19 to remind me to pray 1 Corinthians 6:19. Likewise, you could set an alarm to go off when you know you would normally have a few minutes to stop and pray. Do what works best for you. Whether this concept is foreign to you or a part of your daily practice, give it a try this week.

Day 3
Enlightened through Scripture Study

Pray

Lord, I praise You that there is nothing I could have done that wasn't washed away by Jesus' blood on the cross. Thank You for sending Your Son to die for me. I confess how shame has kept me from seeing myself as You see me and from receiving Your forgiveness and grace. Teach me through Your Word. Help me to accept and embrace that I am worthy of honor. In Jesus' name I pray, amen.

Observe

Passage: Luke 15:11-32 (NIV)

The parable of the prodigal son in Luke 15:11-32, describes 3 main characters: the father, the older son, and the younger son. Contrasts and comparisons often use descriptive language to illustrate a point that helps us remember what we've learned. Use the tool of making lists to help you as you compare and contrast the characters.

o   Make three lists or columns recording everything you learn about the father, the older son, and the younger son.
o   Compare and contrast the characters of the story.
o   Take note of the final outcome for each character.

Interpret

Commentaries are also good resources to use to help you gain further understanding after you have done your own study of a passage. Here are a few things I learned:

o   Hebrew law gave two-thirds inheritance to the oldest son and one-third to the younger.

o   When the Father gave his son a robe, sandals, and a ring, each held great significance. A robe was given to a guest of honor, sandals were only for free men and the son was intending on returning as a slave, and a ring was a symbol of authority. Through these gestures, his father also communicated his lavish love and forgiveness to his son.

o   Now it's your turn. What does it mean to "kill the fattened calf"? Consult a commentary to discover the answer.

o   Record anything else you learn from your commentary research.

Apply/Engage with God

o   If you put yourself in the passage, are you more like the older son or the younger son? Explain why.

o   Look back at your lists and see how you would have ended up in the story. Compare and contrast your life story with the characters. Are there any changes you need to make to rewrite the end of your story?

o   By looking at the father in this passage, what do you learn about how your heavenly Father feels about you and loves you? How does that change how you view yourself?

Enabled through Spiritual Practice

Many of us don't realize the great impact that words have on our lives. One simple word has the power to build up or tear down. Scripture says, *"A person's words can be life-giving water; words of true wisdom are as refreshing as a bubbling brook"* (Proverbs 18:4 NLT). On the contrary, Proverbs 25:18 says, *"Telling lies about others is as harmful as hitting them with an ax, wounding them with a sword or shooting them with a sharp arrow"* (NLT). It is important then that you learn the discipline of controlling your tongue when speaking to others or about others and to yourself or about yourself. Maybe you do a good job in regard to others, but you must be careful to do the same for yourself.

Read the list of words that follow that describe shame and honor. Circle the words that resonate with you in your heart. Don't think too hard about this. Don't judge your answers. Just go with your first thought. Reflect and observe. Which category has more? When these shame words surface, thank God for exposing your shame and bringing it to light. Then write an "I am" statement like I am worthy or I am beloved or I am an heir. Read these statements out loud, every day if you can, to remind yourself who you are in Christ. Ask God to help you control your tongue and begin to honor yourself and others with your words. We will do more with this tomorrow.

HONOR			SHAME		
Accepted	Clothed	Heir	Alien	Enemy	Orphaned
Adopted	Conqueror	Precious	Barren	Enslaved	Poor
Beloved	Exalted	Pure	Blind	Exiled	Rejected
Blessed	Freed	Restored	Cursed	Foolish	Sick
Child	Friend	Resurrected	Dead	Humbled	Stranger
Chosen	Fruit Bearing	Rich	Defeated	Lost	Unknown
Citizen	Glorious	Strong	Defiled	Naked	Unknown
Clean	Healed	Worthy	Dirty	Oppressed	Unworthy

 **Day 4**
Encouraged: Mary's Story

At the age of seven, I stepped into a church for the first time. My four-year-old sister died, and her funeral was at this church. I don't remember many details, for I was living in a fog, but I remember feeling drawn to enter the church building. I was broken and felt empty, yet I wanted to be there. My sister wasn't coming back no matter how hard I wanted her to be with me.

Shortly after the funeral, my mother began to take my brothers and me to church with her. The small church didn't have a lot of children there, and I believe I was the youngest. The Sunday School lessons were hard for me to understand because they were more for the older children. I still felt the pull to be at church every week. By the time I was 12, I knew the basics: Jesus was born in a stable, Jesus died on a cross for my sins, and accept Jesus Christ as my personal savior and I will go to heaven. Sounds easy enough. For me, it was a no-brainer…my sister was in heaven, and of course, I wanted to be with her someday. I accepted Christ.

Life was still full of troubles and consequences. My brothers didn't want to go to church anymore. They said, "Why should we, since Dad doesn't go." My dad hated any social gatherings and was just a quiet man. He never showed emotion or affection and felt uncomfortable with any grouping of people. So I continued to go to church with my mom and was happy to do it. I still felt drawn to church each week.

The choices my brothers were making did not lead to good. In fact, they were quite harmful. They skipped school, smoked, partied, and stole things. I vowed that would not be who I became. I was terrified of consequences…too scared to make a wrong choice. I soon realized it didn't matter how much I wanted to live right, the world broke its way into my life. My brothers were supposed to be watching me while my parents went away for a weekend. Like anything else my parents told them to do, they didn't listen and left me alone to go to a party. I was 14, so I thought it would be all right. But it wasn't.

After midnight, a college student who was at the same party as my brothers came into our house, raped me, and left. Terror rose inside of me and I never felt I would be normal again…broken beyond repair. I didn't know what to do or who to tell. By the time my parents came home, I had convinced myself that I could not tell anyone. My dad said he would kill anyone who touched me, and I didn't want him to go to jail. I had no reason not to believe what he said. It must have been my fault that a 21-year-old man came into our house knowing I was alone and took advantage of me. At 14, I believed this, and to this day, I still struggle with that lie. My parents still do not know about the attack. I made up excuses why it wouldn't benefit anyone if they knew. My father's health isn't good, they would blame themselves, etc.

I didn't understand why this happened to me. God was supposed to protect me, and He didn't. I went to church every week, went faithfully to school and was a good student, accepted Christ…I did all the right things. Why did God allow this? I felt so empty and broken. The guilt and blame I stuffed inside myself blew up in unhealthy living.

My low self-image caused me to make bad choices. I didn't care what I ate because the food comforted me. I also thought that being fat would protect me from being attacked again. This was another lie I believed. I felt unloved and unwanted. Would any man love me? I doubted it. So at the age of 16, I was at a party. Everyone at the party was doing drugs, but when the drugs were offered to me, I said no. I was still a scared, broken girl afraid of consequences and what the drugs might do to me. My refusal of the drugs sparked interest in a man at the party towards me. I thought he was perfect for me…at least he paid attention to me. It was okay that he did drugs, had hair longer than mine, and was an atheist, because I was going to fix him of all these things. By my senior year, I was living with him, and by prom, I was pregnant. I made this all okay in my mind by believing he would now have to stay with me for life and I would have plenty of time to fix him. Believing all of this showed my continual brokenness.

I gave birth to a beautiful baby girl and lived in an abusive marriage. I realized that my daughter's life was in danger by keeping her in this environment and decided to divorce my husband. Failure once again encircled me. I couldn't fix my husband, our house went into foreclosure, and my brokenness continued. I was a failure at everything in my life. I had to get a second job to pay the bills and failed at that too.

After a drawn-out and excruciating divorce, I thought I was finally done with him. Not so. It was finalized when my daughter was four years old. It was a tortuous time. I watched him treat my daughter like he treated me. He manipulated her and filled her with guilt and shame. I did nothing because I thought that she needed to see for herself the monster he was…at four years old. I was broken and failed once again.

Convinced that all men created pain in my life, I thought I would never marry again. I met a man at my second job. As I tried to find a girlfriend for him, he made it clear that it was me he wanted, and we married. He too had a lousy marriage experience and a daughter. He was also broken. There was no counseling that could help us more than God and His Word in our lives. He made it possible for us to have a happy marriage and work on our broken issues. We recommitted our lives to Him and made the Lord the center of our lives. I know He will never leave me or forsake me for He never has. Grace is the glue that is putting the broken pieces together.

Engage with God

- o   How has shame affected your eating and body image struggles?

- o   What parts of Mary's story resonated with you, and what will you do as a result?

Enabled through Spiritual Practice

Refer back to the list of honor/shame words from Day 2. As hard as it may be, thank God for shining His light on your shame and exposing it.

- o   Make a list of all of the shame words you wrote down.
- o   Cross out each shame word and choose an honor word to replace it.
- o   Then, pray the corresponding verse used on the list at the end of the chapter to counteract your shame.
- o   Pick one verse to keep reading every day this week.

 ## Day 5
Entrusted and Empowered

Like the Samaritan woman who sought love and rescue from life's problems in the arms of men, a dark season of life led me into the arms of an eating disorder, hoping it would save me, fix my problems, make me feel loved and accepted. But it was the worst kind of cheater...instead of rescuing me, it enslaved me. I desperately tried to hide it, but my failing health exposed my secret. My pride could hardly bare the looks of surprise, disappointment, and disapproval I received. I lost friends over it. I lost my spark for life. I lost myself in the midst of it. My shame encompassed me. It became hard to discern truth from the lies. I felt hopeless and alone. I longed for someone to come along and rescue me from the darkness that engulfed me. No one ever did. Then one day in my desperation, I cried out to the Lord and He heard my cry. His light exposed the darkness and freed me from my shame, my strongholds, my sin just like He did for the Samaritan woman. I walked away from that moment with dignity just like she did because I was transformed from being known as a sinner to a sinner saved by grace. Why am I telling you my story? Not because I'm proud of it but because it's important that we testify just like the Samaritan woman did in the story. Take a look.

After her encounter with Jesus, the Samaritan woman went back into the village where she was scorned and told the townspeople what happened to her that day. *"Many of the Samaritans from that town believed in Him because of her testimony, 'He told me everything I ever did'"* (John 4:39 NIV). Her story was so compelling that the townspeople went out to meet Jesus. After a while, they said, *"We no longer believe just because of what you said; now we have heard for ourselves and we know that this man really is the Savior of the world"* (John 4:42 NIV). See, her testimony made others come to know or desire to know Jesus.

Your testimony is important too. Maybe you're thinking: You wouldn't say that if you knew my story, or I couldn't, what will others think of me if they knew, or I'm in the midst of my trial now so I'll wait until it's better, or I couldn't do that; I'll mess up the whole thing.

Lies. All lies.

Don't let the enemy persuade you to keep silent. Your testimony only needs to do one thing: invite others into personal contact with Jesus and then Jesus does the rest. Mark 13:11 says, *"Do not worry beforehand about what you are to say, but say whatever is given you in that hour, for it is not you who speak, but it is the Holy Spirit."* This woman was in the thick of it and everybody knew her backstory. But when she proclaimed the Messiah, she allowed God to use her story to transform her whole town. Imagine what could happen if you allow God to use yours?

Engage with God

o   You have a story to tell; are there any barriers keeping you from telling it?

o   Is there anyone in your life with whom God may be prompting you to share your testimony?

Enabled through Spiritual Practice

Undoubtedly, the lesson stirred up some raw emotions surrounding the things in your life for which you feel shame. *"It is for freedom Christ has set us free. Stand firm, then and do not let yourselves be burdened again by a yoke of slavery"* (Galatians 5:1 NIV). The shed blood of Jesus Christ covers you. When God looks at you, He sees the blood of Jesus covering you, not your sins. Prayerfully consider the magnitude of this truth.

Are you carrying around a weighty backpack filled with shame? Don't let shame have a hold over you. Take a few minutes to think about the areas in your life where you feel shame. Then, on the notecard provided list them briefly. In order to symbolically sever the attachment, bring your notecard to the front, and set it on fire. As it burns, remember…

> *"As far as the east is from the west, so far has he removed our transgressions from us"* (Psalm 103:12 NIV).
>
> *"Those who look to him for help will be radiant with joy; no shadow of shame will darken their faces"* (Psalm 34:5 NLT).
>
> *"Instead of your shame you will receive a double portion, and instead of disgrace you will rejoice in your inheritance"* (Isaiah 61:7 NIV).
>
> *"God delights in you, he will quiet you with his love, he will rejoice over you with singing"* (Zephaniah 3:17).

While burning your shame is a powerful image, be sure to double check with the building supervisor ahead of time as to what the fire policies are and make plans accordingly.

Honor Words and Verses	
Accepted	Romans 15:7 – *"Therefore accept one another just as Christ also accepted us."*
Adopted	Romans 8:15 – *"For you have not received a spirit of slavery leading to fear again, but you have received a spirit of adoption as sons by which we cry out, Abba, Father!"*
Beloved	Deuteronomy 33:12 – *"May the beloved of the LORD dwell in security by Him, who shields him all day and he dwells between His shoulders."*
Blessed	Deuteronomy 28:3-8 – *"You will be blessed in the city and blessed in the country. the fruit of your womb will be blessed, and the crops of your land and the young of your livestock… Your basket and your kneading trough will be blessed. You will be blessed when you come, and you go out… The Lord will send a blessing on your barns and on everything you put your hand to. The LORD your God will bless you in the land He is giving you."*
Child	Romans 8:16-17 – *"The Spirit Himself, testifies with our spirit that we are children of God and if children, heirs also, heirs of God and fellow heirs with Christ, if indeed we suffer with Him so that we may also be glorified with Him."*
Chosen	1 Peter 2:9 – *"But you are a chosen people, a royal priesthood, a holy nation, God's special possession, that you may declare the praises of Him who called you out of darkness and into His wonderful light."*
Citizen	Philippians 3:20 – *"But our citizenship is in heaven. And we eagerly await a Savior from there, the LORD Jesus Christ."*
Clean	Hebrews 10:22 – *"Let us draw near with a sincere heart in full assurance of faith, having our hearts sprinkled clean from an evil conscience and our bodies washed with pure water."*
Clothed	Proverbs 31:25 – *"She is clothed with strength and dignity."*
Conqueror	Romans 8:37 – *"In all these things we are more than conquerors through Him who loved us."*
Exalted	Isaiah 52:13 – *"My servant will act wisely; he will be raised, lifted up and highly exalted."*
Freed	John 8:36 – *"So if the Son sets you free, you will be free indeed."*
Friend	James 2:23 – *"And the Scripture was fulfilled that says, 'Abraham believed God and it was credited to him as righteousness, and he was called God's friend.'"*
Fruit Bearing	John 15:8 – *"This is to my Father's glory, that you bear much fruit, showing yourselves to be my disciples."*
Glorious	Colossians 1:27 – *"To them God has chosen to make known among the Gentiles the glorious riches of this mystery, which is Christ in you, the hope of glory."*
Healed	Exodus 15:26 – *"…for I am the LORD who heals you."*
Heir	Romans 8:16-17 – *"The Spirit Himself, testifies with our spirit that we are children of God and if children, heirs also, heirs of God and fellow heirs with Christ, if indeed we suffer with Him so that we may also be glorified with Him."*
Precious	Psalm 116:15 – *"Precious in the sight of the LORD."*
Pure	Psalm 51:10 – *"Create in me a pure heart, O God, and renew a steadfast spirit within me."*
Restored	Psalm 23:3 – *"He restores my soul."*
Resurrected	Romans 6:4 – *"We are therefore buried with Him through baptism into death in order that just as Christ was raised from the dead through the glory of the Father, we too may live a new life."*
Worthy	Matthew 6:26 – *"Look at the birds of the air; they neither sow nor reap nor gather into barns and yet your Heavenly Father feeds them. Are you not of more value than they?"*

ENDNOTES

1   Brené Brown, *The Gift of Imperfect Parenting: Raising Children with Courage, Compassion and Connection* (Audible Audiobook: Sounds True, 2013).

2   Nathaniel Hawthorne, The Scarlet Letter (Toronto, ON:Bantam Classics, Penguin Random House, 1981).

3   Max Lucado, *An Advocate*. Available online at maxlucado.com 15 May 2019.

4   Holley Gerth, blogpost: "Psst…I'm intimidated by you." Available online at *holleygerth.com*, 22 Oct 2014.

Transformed: From Bitter to Forgiving

Day 1
Enlisted to Expose the Darkness

A trip to the jungles of Peru a few years ago broadened my perspective of God's creation in unexpected ways. As I left civilization and entered into the majestic unknown of the jungle, I was impacted by its beauty and power. As I walked through the jungle, beauty was not just something for the eye to behold, it was an experience that engaged all five of my senses simultaneously. As I gazed upon exotic birds, animals, and vegetation, I was struck anew as I thought about God as the Creator, how He took delight and care in designing every detail of the jungle and how much more He delighted in creating me and you.

I also gained new awareness of God's power as Creator. We live very comfortable lives in the 21st century and act more like rulers striving to dominate nature rather than being submissive to it. When I stepped into the jungle, the towering trees, vast foliage, a cacophony of creature sounds quickly engulfed me, making it very clear who was in charge here, and it wasn't me. I became reliant on my guide to discern for me where it was safe to step, which creatures were deadly, and which plants were poisonous.

I learned quickly that I could not spot potential dangers just based on how they appeared. Many of the "dangerous" species were beautiful to behold, and one such creature is the poison dart frog. Though only 2 inches in size, this brightly adorned frog is an eye-catching beauty, yet some of these frogs carry enough deadly poison to kill ten men. It struck me that the same was true for mankind. External beauty is no reflection of the heart. I'm sure we can all think of someone in our lives whose beauty may be striking but their words are like poisonous venom. *"For the mouth speaks what the heart is full of"* (Luke 6:45 NIV). When you allow bitterness to grow in your heart, its ugliness begins to transform you from the inside out. Let the things of God grow in your heart instead, allowing God to do the transformative work.

Engage with God

o   Is there someone in your life whose bitterness is making your life toxic, and what's it like being around them?

o   Are there any boundaries you need to set in order to keep their toxicity from spilling over into your life?

Enabled through Spiritual Practice

I want to applaud you for all the work you have been doing each week as you prayerfully examine the depths of your heart. Such hard and courageous work! I pray it has allowed you to uncover new layers of understanding, healing, and freedom in your life. I imagine it has also uncovered and exposed inner wounds that need healing that only God can give. Friar Richard Rohr suggests why this kind of work is so important. He says:

> "…Pain that is not transformed is transmitted. Untransformed pain leaks onto others. We kick the dog, yell at the kids, oversleep, overeat or numb ourselves to TV—but the pain is still there."[1]

These wounds, while painful to look at and deal with must be addressed in order to keep bitterness from growing. I pray His healing work will continue and bring you newfound freedom in the process.

Using the spiritual discipline of self-examination coupled with journaling, you are invited to explore the depths of your heart on the topic of bitterness within the safety of God's love. You could do an exercise like this for any of the topics we've covered. Sometime this week, carve out some space in your day for an extended journaling time. The question prompts are written at the end of Day 2, but feel free to do them at any point in the week.

Day 2
Entangled by Sin

Just as the poison dart frog gave us a picture of how beauty can conceal the truth and what the overflow of a bitter heart can produce, the matador vine gives us a picture of how bitterness grows. This plant is also found deep in the jungles of South America. What's unique about this vine is that it takes root in the crevasses of the tree and slowly begins to grow. As it grows, its tendrils slowly wrap around the tree clasping tighter and tighter as the vine climbs skyward eventually killing the tree. Once the vine reaches the top, a single flower blossoms and scatters its seeds, starting the process over again. This parasitic, silent destroyer slowly takes over the tree as it grows, suffocating, strangling any remaining life. The matador vine does to a tree what bitterness does to a heart. Not a pretty picture.

No one ever sets out to become bitter. In order to uncover how bitterness grows, let's look at how it develops. The first step in the process usually begins when you feel wronged. Maybe you are a victim of abuse and your abuser isn't sorry. Maybe something was taken from you unjustly and you want it back. Maybe you are angry with God because he allowed a tragedy to occur in your life. Maybe you can forgive others, but you can't forgive yourself for what you have done. Maybe you are angry and don't want to forgive. Maybe you want to take matters into your own hands and get revenge, restitution, and justice instead.

Situations like these can breed feelings of anger, jealousy, hatred, fear, shame, and distrust. When these feelings aren't dealt with and deep-seated hurts are unresolved, the soil is ripe to plant seeds of unfor-giveness in our hearts. When unforgiveness isn't challenged and weeded out but instead is allowed to grow, it can slowly overtake the garden of our heart just like the matador vine can overtake a tree. What a powerful picture of how allowing unforgiveness to grow can destructively permeate every aspect of our lives and, eventually, overtake our hearts and form roots of bitterness.

If not dealt with, bitterness continues to grow and consumes more of our soul than we realize it ever could. Bitterness leaks and oozes from us in ugly ways with surprising venom like the poison dart frog. It's contagious and it spreads to others just like the matador vine flower scatters its seeds all around. Unlike the poison dart frog, this poison hurts you and those around you. Like Senator Alan Simpson quoted his mother saying:

> *"Hatred corrodes the container it's carried in."*[2]

Clinical research documents that bitterness directly affects our mental health and often leads to depres-sion, anxiety, and anger issues. Likewise, its effects can be seen in our physical health, often manifesting itself through cardiovascular issues, a weakened immune system, and high blood pressure.

Bitterness also inhibits our spiritual growth and hinders God's love from flowing through us into the lives of others. It never solves or resolves our problems even though we think it should. The enemy takes advantage of these toxic feelings, using every opportunity to turn our focus away from God and onto ourselves. It drives us to desperately seek comfort and refuge in the arms of things that numb our pain, like eating disorders, alcohol, drugs, sex, and the like. While these may offer temporary relief, they slowly and subtly entrench us even deeper and further into destructive patterns. If this is how you feel, you may be asking yourself, "How did I get here?" and "How do I get out of here?"

Acknowledge and grieve the loss. The first step toward healing is to acknowledge that the pain and loss you feel is real. The loss may be so great that it feels like an amputation. Instead of longing for the limb to grow back or ruminating on how you lost it, accept it as a loss and try finding a way forward by learn-ing how to function with it no longer there. Give yourself space to process and come to grips with your feelings. Sometimes these feelings are too big and overwhelming for us to handle alone. Tell a friend, counselor, or pastor what you are experiencing and let them walk beside you in your grief.

Confess your feelings. Remember your feelings themselves are not wrong, but ignoring, justifying, minimizing, or denying them can open a door to the enemy. By not dealing with them, you allow the person who wronged you to continue to hold power over you and to hurt you over and over again by reliving what was done in the past. To keep Satan from obtaining a foothold in your life through your feelings over the matter, try confessing them instead of concealing them. Confession helps you to turn to God with your feelings and deal with them in a godly way. It also helps to dial down the intensity of your emotions so that you can see beyond the hurt. While the garden of your heart may still bare the scars of your wounds for quite some time, it can still flourish when the weed of bitterness is removed.

Forgive yourself and those who have hurt you. Even if the person who wronged you is not sorry, you are still called to forgive and that includes yourself. Forgiveness is about your own heart and keeping it undefiled. In the short term, withholding forgiveness gives you a sense of restitution, justice, or power and control over the other person. But in the long run, it just eats away at your own heart, hurting you, not them. This doesn't mean you have to forgive and forget like it never happened. Forgiveness does not mean that you must excuse or accept the evil act, in fact, God says you should "hate what is evil; cling to what is good" (Romans 12:9). Instead, God calls you to forgive, not to excuse the wrongs that have happened but so that unforgiveness has no room to grow in you to your own detriment.

Jerry Sittser, in his book *A Grace Disguised*, chronicles his journey of grief, loss, and forgiveness after he witnessed his mother, wife, and daughter tragically killed by a drunk driver. He says this about forgiveness:

> *"The process of forgiveness begins when victims realize that nothing—not justice or revenge or anything else—can reverse the wrong done. Forgiveness cannot spare victims the consequences of the loss, nor can it recover the life they once had. Victims have no power to change the past...they can choose to stop the cycle of destruction and, in the wake of wrong done, do what is right. Forgiveness is simply choosing to do the right thing."[3]*

What about justice? God is a God of both justice and forgiveness. Forgiveness is a personal act that purifies our heart while justice for wrongs done lies in the hands of God. How do we reconcile this when the unforgivable has been done? Rachael Denhollander, the first of more than a hundred women to publicly accuse Larry Nassar of sexual abuse, describes justice and forgiveness in this way:

> *"Justice is positively defined as being what is merited or deserved meaning justice for me and for my abuser is that we get what we deserve. This is where we start to feel the tension between Justice and forgiveness. Because if we accept that Justice is conformity to an absolute standard of goodness set by God this is a good thing, a right thing.*
>
> *"Forgiving is also held out in Scripture as a Christian virtue, and we are commanded to pursue it as well....So, forgiveness is giving up resentment. It's giving up a claim to retaliation, a claim to injure my abuser the way he injured me."*

She goes on to say what God has promised to us who seek justice:

> *"God has promised not only eternal justice, but He's also provided earthly means for us to pursue it. This is where the Christian faith portrays the most beautiful and true picture of both justice and forgiveness, the lion and the lamb."[4]*

I invite you to view the entire message from Rachael Denhollander at https://www.youtube.com/watch?v=AZsA8tur_Ik (starting a 17:50-20:48).

Pray for those who hurt you. Don't lose sight of the fact that the person who wronged you is also a child of God. Maybe they did the unthinkable and it was wrong, but God still offers them grace and mercy even though they don't deserve it. Jesus illustrated this when the teachers of the law brought to Him a woman caught in the act of adultery, saying the law states she is to be stoned. Jesus response was, *"Let any of you who is without sin be the first to throw a stone at her"* (John 8:7 NIV). No one stoned the woman because they realized they were not without sin either. Don't forget you are a sinner saved by grace too. Remember, our forgiveness doesn't excuse, minimize, approve, or erase what happened. Rather it acknowledges our own sinful nature, that we are also sinners, and that God sent His Son to die for all of us to atone for our sins.

Forgive because God forgives. In His Sermon on the Mount, Jesus says this, *"For if you forgive other people when they sin against you, your Heavenly Father will also forgive you. But if you do not forgive the sins of others your Heavenly Father will not forgive your sins"* (Matthew 6:14-15). Forgiveness is truly a matter of the heart. God lavishly extends love, mercy, and compassion on us when we ask for forgiveness, no matter what we've done, so that we can turn around and do the same for others. God was willing to forgive you when you didn't deserve it; are you willing to forgive others in that same way?

Engage with God/Enabled through Spiritual Practice

We're going to combine our reflection and individual practice with an extended journaling time. Journaling gives us the opportunity to process, struggle, identify, and empty our hearts before the Lord. There is no right or wrong way to do it. There is only one rule: be honest. As you review what you wrote, don't judge it by thinking you should or shouldn't feel this way. Instead, allow the insights you gained to become a starting point for your conversation with the Lord. Start with prayer and ask the Lord to bring to mind what He wants you to reflect on.

1. Are there people in your life who have wronged you? List their names.
2. Looking at the list, ask the Lord for one person to focus on for this exercise and circle it. Briefly describe the circumstances when you felt wronged by this person and the outcome.
3. Have you forgiven this person? Explain why or why not?
4. What emotions does remembering these events evoke in you? Don't edit, just write.
5. Did anything you wrote down surprise you? Explain. Remember feelings are not wrong. In fact, they give you important information.
6. Have you ever talked about those feelings with God? Give it a try.
7. Are harboring unforgiveness or bitterness in your heart towards the person? How do you know? Invite God into the conversation.
8. How do you think holding unforgiveness and bitterness in your heart affects you or others around you? Describe.
9. How do your past hurts affect your relationship with that person?
10. Are you holding any unforgiveness towards yourself because of what happened with this person? Why or why not?
11. Has this person played a role in your eating and body image struggles? How?
12. What steps might God be asking you to take towards forgiving them?
13. Let's shift gears, think of the worst thing you have ever done. Just go with the first thing that comes to mind. Briefly describe what happened and the outcome.

14. What emotions does remembering these events evoke in you?
15. Did anything surprise you?
16. Have you ever talked about these feelings with God? Give it a try.
17. Are you harboring unforgiveness in your heart towards yourself for the choices you've made?
18. What is keeping you from forgiving yourself?
19. Has an inability to forgive yourself influenced how you see yourself? Describe how.
20. Has unforgiveness of yourself contributed to your eating and body image struggles? Describe how.
21. What might God want you to know about how He sees you? Ask Him and record what you learn.
22. Do you think you deserve forgiveness? Why or why not?
23. Do you deserve forgiveness any more than the person who hurt you?
24. What might God want you to know about forgiveness?
25. What steps might the Lord be asking you to take to forgive yourself?

Day 3
Enlightened through Scripture Study

Pray

Lord, I don't want my heart to end up overcome by bitterness like a matador vine overcomes a tree. Root out any areas of unforgiveness in my heart so that I can grow. Thank You that no sin is too great for You to forgive. Thank You for the forgiveness You so freely extend to Your children. Teach me how to forgive like You forgive. In Jesus' name I pray, amen.

Observe

Passage: Matthew 18:21-35 (NIV)

God teaches us about forgiveness in the parable of the unmerciful servant found in Matthew 18:21-35.

- o Look for the repeated word/concept of forgive/forgiveness. Mark each reference to the word in the same way.
- o Using the tool of word study,
  - o Look up the Greek word for *debt* in verse 27 and compare it with the Greek word used for *debt* in verse 32.
  - o Look up the Greek word for *take pity on, cancelled* (v. 27), *mercy* (v. 33) and any other words that stand out to you. Record what you learn.
  - o Compare and contrast your findings. Record what you learn.
- o Using the tool of making lists, do a character study: In this parable, the king (figuratively God) has decided to settle his accounts with servants who had borrowed money from him. Record what you learn about the King, his servant, and his fellow servant as they are described in the passage.

Interpret

Understanding the historical context of a passage can bring new insight and meaning.

- o Look up the significance of the forgiving 7 times vs. Jesus saying 77 times. What would Rabbinic law during that time have required for repeated sin?
- o Convert 10 thousand bags of gold and 100 silver coins to today's equivalents. How does this change your perspective on the debt forgiven?

Refer back to your character study. Compare and contrast the relationships between master/servant and servant/fellow servant.

- o What do you learn about the King/Master's character?
- o What do you learn about the servant's character?

Apply/Engage with God

- o How do you respond to people when they wrong you? Do you respond more like the master cancelling debt no matter how great? Or, are you more like the servant who, even though he has been forgiven much, is unwilling to extend that same forgiveness to others?

- o In light of what you learned in this passage, what is God asking you to do regarding the people you find hard to forgive?

Enabled through Spiritual Practice

In your journaling time, did God reveal to you someone towards whom you are holding bitterness in your heart? Jesus challenges us to *"love our enemies and pray for those who persecute you"* (Matthew 5:44). You're probably thinking, "Who can really do that?" Without God's help, we cannot. Confess your feelings towards this person to the Lord and ask Him to erase the bitterness from your heart and rewrite truth over top of it.

In an effort to let God change our hearts towards our enemies, imagine what it must be like to walk in their shoes. Let us commit to praying a prayer of intercession for them every day this week with this visual reminder. Stand on a piece of construction paper. Trace your feet and then cut out the paper footsteps. It may be hard to find words at first, so write out a few verses on your cutouts that you can pray over them. Then put the feet in a place that will remind you to pray each day and see how God changes your heart.

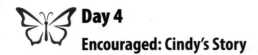
Day 4
Encouraged: Cindy's Story

I didn't think there was a problem until the comments about my shrinking waistline began to turn from compliments to concern. I ate healthy and ran. I was proud of my accomplishments and my ability to say no to things that majority culture told me were unhealthy or "bad" foods, but over time, my desire to be healthy transitioned into a restrictive and unhealthy relationship with food.

I had grown up in a stable, loving, and Christian home. I had a Christian education and a strong support system, including family, friends, and church leaders. I would describe my growing up as "normal" with little disruption or drama.

My "normal" life changed in 2008 when I was in seventh grade. I remember the night my parents sat my sister and me down and explained my mom had been diagnosed with breast cancer. Not knowing what to think or feel, I stuffed this new piece of information into the back of my mind and continued living life as usual. My mom was sick for a few years and, not wanting chemotherapy, tried various natural methods and treatments to fight the cancer. Her treatment was highly dependent on a specific diet that included items such as wheat grass, flax seed, and organic produce. My mother began making more healthy meals for the whole family, introducing me to this new world of natural (or clean) eating.

My mom's condition did not improve and in the summer of 2011, she passed away. Her actual death did not seem to hurt too much since I had already lost her as the disease infected her brain. The mom I had known had slowly faded away. By this time, I was already deep in isolation, taking on the role of "mom" for my family, and assuming responsibilities such as grocery shopping, cleaning, and taking care of my younger brother—all in addition to my schoolwork. Alongside this, I was using exercise as an outlet to release all the pent-up anger I felt. I excused the disordered behavior and eating as my attempt to take care of myself and control my feelings. No one questioned me, so I kept going.

During this time, my dad began dating. It was fine at first, but as he became more serious with a woman, my anger and bitterness grew. I didn't want my mom to be replaced, or my dad to be preoccupied with someone else. During this dating period, I lost a significant amount of weight and was proud of it. Fitness was under my control even though my dad's new relationship was not. Two years after my mom's passing my dad got remarried. At the wedding, an adult family friend approached me and asked if I was okay. She was concerned about my health because I looked so thin and wondered if I might have an eating disorder. This infuriated and confused me, but it was after this episode that I started to consider that my eating/exercise patterns were abnormal and possibly life-threatening.

It took me a while to come to terms with the fact that I struggled with anorexia, but after doing some research, things lined up. I had lost my period, I was consumed with thoughts about food, I checked the scale almost daily, I avoided full food groups and used exercise to compensate for any calories taken in. I later realized that my eating disorder was a way for me to cope with the anger and negative feelings I had in response to the two big unwanted life changes that occurred so close together. I was grasping for control.

My senior year flew by and I half-enjoyed the fun events and senior trips, but my eating disorder blocked me from fully engaging. Scared to be around food, I didn't like to attend social events. My prom created stress because I was self-conscious of my thin arms and protruding collarbone, and I still harbored unforgiveness toward my dad, mom, step-mom, and God. By the time I graduated I was ready to run away to college, forget my struggles, and do my own thing.

But God had other plans. During the years of my mom's sickness, death, and my dad's remarriage, I didn't really acknowledge God. I still called myself a Christian and admired my mom for her strong faith during great hardship, but my faith was not doing anything for me. I would outwardly affirm that God had a reason and plan in all my loss, but my life reflected my hardness of heart toward Him. I was not living the abundant life that God offered me.

So, before I made the mistake of going off to college in my unhealthy state, God threw me a lifeline. My mom's twin sister from Colorado came for my graduation party and offered for me to come live with her. As a strong woman of God who is attentive to people's needs, she noticed my struggle and offered her home as a place where I could be discipled and nourished both spiritually and physically.

I initially said no. I was going to college and nothing was going to change that, but God changed my heart. A few weeks after graduation, I bought my plane ticket to Colorado knowing I was stepping into some of the hardest days of my life. I went willingly, knowing that God had more in store for me.

My year in Colorado was the hardest yet greatest season of my life. God tore down all my walls and preconceived ideas of who God is and rebuilt me in Christ. I learned the freedom that comes with letting go. My desire to be healed grew as I saw an example of what an abundant life looked like.

I had to willingly put myself under the spiritual authority and discipleship of my aunt and uncle and allowed my aunt to determine my meal plan. I began to see physical improvements and steady increase toward overall health. I spent time volunteering in the community and began to step out faithfully where God called me. As my faith and confidence in God grew, I was less preoccupied with food and exercise, and I saw other areas of my life fall into place.

After a year of living in Colorado, my recovery was underway and I was consistently maintaining health. I still had some disordered thoughts but wasn't acting on them, largely because I had learned how to fight off the lies with the truth of God's Word. I felt spiritually and physically strong as I left Colorado and began college.

I entered college optimistically, even though the transition to college and meeting new people was stressful. As my semesters at school got harder and more chaotic, so did my mind and heart. Following some other deaths in my family and the hard-hitting reality of a full semester, I returned to my old eating and exercising patterns.

Now, still in college, I struggle at times. I feel like my eating disorder is the thorn in my side. Since Colorado, I have been dedicated to fighting for health and total wellness. I do want to get well. I want to be able to serve God and others wholly well. Through the hardship and pain, I have seen God at work. I believe that I already have victory over my eating disorder, but there are currently some barriers keeping me from fully walking in that victory. God is slowly showing me new areas of my life that needs reshaping, and this requires obedience and intentionality. I have hope, knowing that God has forgiven my past and is redeeming all things, including the brokenness within my family and in my heart.

It is frustrating that I have been struggling for so long with an eating disorder, but I acknowledge that God is not finished with me yet. He is molding me and reshaping me. I have learned to reach out for help and not give up on recovery even when it's hard to keep up with appointments and goals. One of my driving forces is knowing God has more in store for me. He has been using me despite my unfaithfulness and brokenness. I want to recover so that I can be better equipped to carry out God's calling on my life: to walk alongside those who are hurting and need healing.

Engage with God

o   How does bitterness affect your eating and body image issues?

o   What parts of Cindy's story resonated with you, and what will you do as a result?

Enabled through Spiritual Practice

Psalm 19:14 says, *"May these words of my mouth and this meditation of my heart be pleasing in your sight, LORD, my Rock and my Redeemer"* (NIV). I get immediate feedback on my words but very rarely anything about the meditations of my heart. Try this exercise and see what God reveals to you about the meditations of your heart.

If you are anything like me, your mind can wander during prayer time. My thoughts bounce from the permission slip I forgot to sign to an item to add to my grocery list to the email I wanted to send before bouncing back to my prayer focus. I used to berate myself until I learned the tool of recollection prayer. Instead of dismissing them, I acknowledge them and write the thought down taking only a few words to describe it and go back to prayer. This does two things; it allows me to let go of the thought (and not forget what I need to do later). It also gives me the opportunity to look back over my list and see if any patterns of thinking emerge. It might reveal a deeper layer of fear, anxiety, idols, lies, shame, and the like, lurking beneath the surface that needs to be addressed and/or confessed.

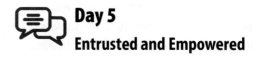 ## Day 5
Entrusted and Empowered

We started off our week using scenes from the jungles of South America as metaphors for our spiritual lives. The Bible often uses imagery from nature to explain biblical principles since that was something familiar and relatable to the audience at that time. In the Parable of the Sower (Mark 4, Matthew 13, Luke 8), Jesus describes the effectiveness of four different types of soil for growing crops as a metaphor for the soil of our hearts for spiritual growth (see Mark 4:1-20). Any gardener knows that plants need water and care every day in order to grow. If neglected, the plant does not thrive and dies. Likewise, intentional care of the soil of your heart will cause you to grow and flourish in the things of God. What kind of soil are you cultivating in your heart?

Maybe it's time to *"break up the unplowed ground"* (Hosea 10:12 NIV) and get to work on the soil of your heart. God gives three instructions for how to do this in regard to bitterness. First is to *"get rid of all bitterness…be kind and compassionate…forgiving each other, just as in Christ God forgave you"* (Ephesians 4:31-32 NIV). Take careful inventory of what is in your heart, and if you find bitterness there, get rid of it! Ask God to help you take steps to replace it with kindness, compassion, and forgiveness.

Second is to *"see to it…that no bitter root grows up to cause trouble and defile many"* (Hebrews 12:15 NIV). Once bitterness has been removed, see to it that it does not take root again. That may involve putting safeguards in place. Just like we put a fence around our garden to keep unwanted predators out, what things can you put in place to guard your heart from the enemy? Recollection prayer is a helpful exercise to attend to the soil of our hearts by means of confession and forgiveness, which will keep bitterness from taking root again.

Third is to live our lives *"rooted and built up in Him"* (Colossians 2:6-7). Once our soil is prepared, sinful roots have been removed and a sturdy fence is in place, it's time to sow seeds of righteousness. Hosea 10:12 says, *"Sow righteousness for yourselves, reap the fruit of unfailing love, and break up your unplowed ground"* (NIV). These new seeds help ensure that our root structure is firmly established and built up in the things of God, not the things of this world. Then when the heat of trials come, your leaves will always be green (Jeremiah 17:8 NIV), because your roots run deep into the streams of life.

Friend, don't let your past define your present. Don't let the poison of bitterness permeate you and keep you from all that God has for you. Lay it down and allow God to remove bitterness from your heart so that the other seeds of love, grace, and contentment may grow without being choked by the weeds of bitterness.

Engage

o   What kind of soil are you cultivating in your heart?

o   How can you tangibly walk out the three instructions in Hosea 10:12 – 1) sowing seeds of righteousness, 2) reaping the fruit of unfailing love and, 3) breaking up the unplowed ground?

Enabled through Spiritual Practice

Sometimes our wounds go so deep that we are too overwhelmed, weak, and exhausted to pray for ourselves. When this happens, we can be sure that even when *"we do not know what to pray for, the Spirit*

Himself intercedes for us through wordless groans" (Romans 8:26 NIV). Take comfort in that promise. However, don't be afraid to ask for some prayer support from a trusted friend, pastor, or family member. God promises that wherever *"two or three gather in my name, there am I with them"* (Matthew 18:20 NIV). You could even consider meeting with one of them regularly to pray over your needs and the needs of your friends, family, church, and beyond.

There is power in praying with others. James 5:13-16 offers further insight into healing prayer; it says the following:

> *"Is anyone among you in trouble? Let them pray. Is anyone happy? Let them sing songs of praise. Is anyone among you sick? Let them call the elders of the church to pray over them and anoint them with oil in the name of the LORD. And the prayer offered in faith will make the sick person well; the LORD will raise them up. If they have sinned, they will be forgiven. Therefore, confess your sins to each other and pray for each other so that you may be healed. The prayer of a righteous person is powerful and effective"* (NIV).

My church takes this passage very seriously and offers elder prayer on a monthly basis. The elders pray in faith on behalf of anyone who comes to them. Simply coming under the authority of the elders and confessing to them your prayer needs is an act of obedience that opens your heart to God and brings healing. I have had the privilege of going myself and accompanying many women to elder prayer, to stand with them, and pray for them when they no longer have the words to pray. I have witnessed God doing amazing healing works in their lives—sometimes physically, sometimes spiritually, sometimes mentally, sometimes quickly, and sometimes slowly. God answers your prayers in His way and timing. Your job is to come before Him in faith and give Him the opportunity to heal you. Consider scheduling a time of healing prayer, whether it's at your church or in your community. He can't heal you or free you if you don't ask.

ENDNOTES

1   Friar Richard Rohr, *Things Hidden: Scripture as Spirituality* (Franciscan Media: 2008), 24.
2   Alan Simpson, Euology of George H. W. Bush Sr., 5 Dec, 2018.
3   Jerry Sitzer, *A Grace Disguised: How the Soul Grows Through Loss* (Grand Rapids, MI: Zondervan, 2004), 141.
4   Rachael Denhollander, "A Time to Speak: Addressing Justice and Forgiveness," Speech given in Grand Rapids, MI, 13 Feb 2019.

Session 12
Transformed: From Isolated to United

Day 1
Enlisted to Expose the Darkness

Last year my husband, an otherwise healthy man in his mid-forties, was diagnosed with cancer. The news blindsided us. Further testing led to the discovery of a second, unrelated cancer in his kidney. Another blow. This was particularly surprising because my husband is a urologist. Not only is kidney cancer his surgical specialty, it has also been the focus of his medical research for nearly two decades. Suddenly our lives came to a screeching halt. Our world was turned upside down as a treatment plan was mapped out making the next six months look drastically different than what we had planned. If that wasn't enough, during that same time, we had a water leak in our kitchen forcing us to replace all of the main level flooring, a close family friend died, and our son started having some health problems as well. I felt overwhelmed wondering how I would shoulder this burden alone.

I didn't have to worry. As the news spread within our community, the response was overwhelming. Friends, family, neighbors, church members, coworkers, school teachers, and the like, began to pray, support, and encourage each member of our family. They offered to help provide rides, meals, redecorating, caregiving, companionship, entertainment, and anything else we might need. To be loved, surrounded, cared for so lavishly on this unexpected detour was a gift from God. Experiencing firsthand community at its best, helped me understand God's design for community and it was beautiful.

Unfortunately, not all communities respond in this way as their members walk in the valley. While most can champion cancer, not everyone knows what to do with separation, divorce, affairs, abuse, addictions, death of a child, eating disorders, and betrayal. They don't know what to say, how to help, and don't want to "take sides" often creating emotional distance, making the valley a lonely place to walk.

I know relationships and community are God's design, but let's be honest, relationships can be problematic, complicated, even hurtful. Selfishness, sin, and our own evil desires mar our relationships. Because relationships require trust, once that trust is betrayed and broken, it is difficult to restore, which makes us less willing to enter into both new and old relationships for fear of being hurt again.

This week we will explore the different aspects of community. Community isn't always easy but know that God can still use relationships to teach us, humble us, refine us, and even smooth our rough edges.

Engage

o   What has been your greatest struggle and your greatest blessing from being in community?

o   When something difficult happens, do you tend to reach out for help or withdraw?

o   Thinking back to previous sessions, how do lies, fear, idolatry, perfectionism, and shame play a role in your desire to withdraw or isolate?

Enabled through Spiritual Practice

God designed us for life with others, and we will explore some ways to do that this week through the spiritual disciplines of small group, accountability partners, mentoring, and utilizing spiritual gifts. However, first we need to start by taking inventory of the most important relationship in our lives, our relationship with God. Since healthy relationships with others flow out of our relationship with God, when God is not on the throne of our heart, our relationships suffer. How easily other people, jobs, material things, money, and success slowly usurp and become more important to us than God. The discipline of detachment invites us to identify anyone or anything in our lives that has taken God's place as first in our hearts so that we can make the necessary changes to restore Him to His proper place.

Start by making a list of what is most important to you including people, places, things, and status. Ask God to reveal to you any areas that have knowingly or unknowingly usurped His role as first in your heart. Confess how you have become more attached to them than to Him. Release and surrender each area to Him, trusting God with it to bring forth something better than you could have accomplished on your own. Receive God's grace and forgiveness. Ask God to help you form a better, stronger attachment to Him and to teach you how to trust Him to do that in every area of your life. Spend some time praising God and thanking Him for the work He has done and will do in your life as a result

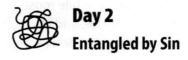

Day 2
Entangled by Sin

In order to better understand God's design for community, let's look at three different aspects: isolation, solitude, and community.

Isolation

When Miriam was stricken with leprosy, Numbers 12:15 says she was *"isolated outside the camp for seven days"* (ISV).[1] Other translations use phrases like "confined," "kept outside," and "shut outside" to describe her place outside the camp. Isolation here means more than just being alone—it carries negative connotations with it. The word implies that Miriam was removed, quarantined, exiled, shunned, even ostracized from her community because of her disease. What shame, rejection, abandonment, anger, and fear she must have experienced as a result of being cast out of the camp during those seven days.

Miriam didn't have a choice when she was put outside the camp, but I did. As my eating disorder gained momentum, I steadily withdrew from my community. I found excuses to not go to social events, meet up for coffee, or keep up with old friends. I became masterful at avoiding direct questions and kept others talking about themselves, sharing less and less of my true thoughts and feelings. I was slowly building a wall around my heart because I was afraid that others would be disappointed at what they found inside there, judge me, abandon me. The increased time alone with my thoughts only allowed the enemy's voice to grow louder and his lies more believable as they played through my mind like a playlist on unending repeat. With my thoughts unchecked, it was harder to discern truth from lies, leaving me more vulnerable to the enemy's tactics. I thought I was protecting myself, when in reality I was opening myself up to spiritual attack by not allowing the body of Christ to point me back to truth. I became an emotional island with very few visitors. Proverbs 18:1 warns, *"Whoever isolates himself seeks his own desire; he breaks out against all sound judgment"* (ESV). Yes, the enemy had me right where he wanted me—alone, disconnected, and afraid.

Because Isolation can open us up to spiritual attack, community helps makes us less vulnerable. God foresaw the dangers associated with isolation. In His infinite wisdom, God designed us to need one another to make our communities optimally function. We see this in 1 Corinthians 12:20-21, *"As it is, there are many parts, but one body. The eye cannot say to the hand 'I don't need you!' And the hand cannot say to the feet, 'I don't need you'"* (NIV). God has given all of us different gifts, talents, and abilities, having equal value and importance and designed to function together. This becomes readily apparent to us when one part of our body ceases to function as it should.

Think about it this way, you might not notice or think about your Achilles tendon very often, but if you injure it, you become very aware of its vital role in every part of your day-to-day functioning. As you recover, you rely more heavily on other parts of your body while your Achilles heals. Likewise, when we are struggling, God designed the church body to rise up and help by picking up some extra slack so that you can heal and recover. That may take the form of intercessory prayer, accompanying you to appointments, eating meals with you, being a shoulder to cry on, or holding you accountable. When we isolate ourselves, we rob the community of their contribution to our lives and its contribution to ours. Are you willing to let the body of Christ walk alongside you in the midst of your struggle?

Solitude

The word *solitude* also describes being alone, but it denotes a vastly different concept than described by the word *isolation*. When in isolation you are focused on yourself. When in solitude you are focused on God. Jesus often retreated in solitude to pray and be alone with God (Mark 1:35, Matthew 14:23). His retreat was temporary, intentional, and often at crucial points in His ministry. From these verses, we learn that time spent alone with God in solitude is biblical, refreshing, and restorative. However, time spent in isolation brings anxiety, depression, loneliness, and fear. The next time you are alone, try focusing upward instead of inward and see what God has in store for you!

My desire to escape to an emotional island did not refresh me; rather, it was a coping mechanism to provide some relief from the overwhelming stress I was experiencing. I was running away. But God doesn't want us to run away, He wants us to run to Him. When Jesus was overcome by the masses who needed healing, the demands of His ministry, and the enormity of the ultimate sacrifice God the Father was asking Him to make on the cross, He sought God alone in prayer. When we run to God and invite Him into our struggles, He transforms isolation into life-giving solitude. Here in solitude you will be reminded of God's promises, His faithfulness, His sovereignty, His path. As you turn to Him, He will refresh you, give you direction, give you comfort, give you peace, restoring and reviving you wherever you need it most.

Community

All of us have had both positive and negative experiences with our community that shaped our view of it, but more importantly, we need to let the Scriptures shape our view of it. In order to better understand God's intentions for community, let's take a look at four different passages of Scripture together.

Designed for companionship. In Genesis 2:18, *"The LORD God said, 'It is not good for man to be alone. I will make a helper suitable for him'"* (NIV). Here we learn that when God was creating the earth and all that is in it, He recognized in His infinite wisdom that in order for man to thrive as He intended, man would need a companion. Likewise, Ecclesiastes 4:9-12 illustrates the benefits of a companion when it says, *"Two are better than one…if either of them falls down, one can help the other up…if two lie down together, they will keep warm…though one may be overpowered, two can defend themselves"* (NIV). Man went from existing to flourishing with the help of a companion. Having others in our lives helps us complete tasks more quickly, keeps us emotionally connected, and makes us more confident in battle knowing someone else has got our backs. That is why it is so helpful to connect with others facing the same challenges as you are in a support group, a Bible study, an online forum, and the like. It's comforting and validating to know others who understand the struggle and can say "me too."

Designed for accountability. James 5:16 instructs us to *"confess your sins to each other and pray for each other so that you may be healed"* (NIV). Nobody likes to admit they are wrong or that they have fallen into sin. However, when we don't confess sin, we leave room for our sinful behaviors and thoughts to grow in the darkness that secrecy provides. We fear the consequences of our sin being revealed, yet over time, the weight of our secrets only leads to more sin and suffering. Confession brings our sin out of darkness and into the light. Accountability keeps us from falling into the same sin again. Whether it's a friend, a counselor, a coach, or group, scheduling regular times to check in on your progress keeps you on your desired path. There may still be consequences as a result of your sin, but now you have a friend to share the load with you, pray for you, and help you through it.

Designed for encouragement. Galatians 6:2 calls us to *"bear one another's burdens, and so fulfill the law of Christ"* (ESV). Our life on God's path is a marathon, not a sprint, so that's why God intended for us to bear one another's burdens. God does not promise us an easy path when we follow Him. My path has included much sorrow and suffering; maybe yours has too. But God placed true burden bearers in my life to walk alongside me at every point of my journey. They comforted me, listened to me, encouraged me, supported me, cried with me, rejoiced with me, spoke truth to me…even when it hurt. I don't know how I could have endured the valleys without these precious friends. They have been the tangible hands of God ministering to me no matter what challenges life has brought.

Designed for unity. Matthew 18:19 tells us *"that if two of you on earth agree about anything they ask for; it will be done for them by my Father in heaven"* (NIV). Our world is full of people with different opinions, ideas, and morals, making it difficult to agree on how to do things. As believers, we might not see eye to eye on everything, but we can agree on the truth of God's Word. God intended for us to pray together and unite. When we stand in agreement and ask God to move on our behalf, we engage in a battle *"against the spiritual forces of evil in the heavenly realms"* (Ephesians 6:12 NIV). When we are up against spiritual forces, we need to call in reinforcements to pray, just as we would in any battle. Let me tell you, if I'm going to wage war against the devil's evil schemes, you bet I'm calling in reinforcements. When we choose to stand on God's promises together and call on the mighty name of Jesus, heaven will respond. There is power when we stand on God's truths, united together, and agreeing in prayer. Otherwise, we pray alone. Pride kept me from admitting how much I was struggling and from asking others to pray for me. Don't let it keep you. The more people who can bombard the gates of heaven on your behalf in prayer, the better.

Companionship, confession, burden sharing, prayer, unity. These are valuable resources God provides for us in our battle against the enemy. When we function like this in our communities, we serve each other the way God intended. It's easier to not confess your sins to one another, to focus on yourself, to go it alone, but when you do, you miss out on all of the blessings God has for you in community. Beloved, stop hiding! Don't be an emotional island with few visitors. Tap into those resources and step out in faith by sharing your struggle with someone. It's time to get off that island!

*Unfortunately, not all communities function as God intended, bringing destruction instead of healing. For more information on toxic relationships and how to deal with them, consult the resource page of the Appendix.

Engage

o   Ask God what He would want you to know about the role isolation, solitude, and community play in your life and record what you learn.

o   How does God's view of community compare to your own preconceived understanding? Are there any changes you need to make?

o   How has social media played a role in developing or destroying your communities?

Enabled through Spiritual Practice

Spending time alone with God refreshes our soul. The quietness of solitude opens up space where God can reveal things to you that you might miss in the business of your everyday life. Set aside some intentional uninterrupted time (15 minutes or more) where you can be alone in the presence of God. Afterwards, reflect on how it was for you to be alone with God. Record your thoughts and anything God revealed to you. Because our culture today is such a stimulating environment, I find it often takes me longer than 15 minutes to be able to empty my mind and feel at rest. Try scheduling a longer period time of several hours to be in solitude with God. I find if I don't schedule it, things always seem to come up, often cutting my solitude time in half.

Disconnect from all technology and set aside your to-do lists. You may have to physically be in a different location so that you are not tempted to do any last-minute things around the house. In order for me to feel released to fully engage in solitude, I need to go to a retreat center. When I say retreat center, I don't mean the kind with speakers, workshops, and other people. This can be a wonderful experience, but it does not give you solitude with God. What I mean is a place where you can go, undistracted, away from others and commune solely with God. Just as in your human relationships, spending time with God grows your relationship with Him. These pockets of time help you unplug from your world and plug into God, allowing you to drink deeply from His waters of life.

Day 3
Enlightened through Scripture Study

Pray

Lord, thank You for being reliable, trustworthy, faithful, and sovereign. Thank You for meeting with me whenever I call upon Your name. I confess the ways that I have isolated myself and run from You instead of to You. Transform those tendencies and create a desire in my heart to run to You. In Jesus' name I pray, amen.

Observe

Passage: 1 Corinthians 12:12-27 (NASB)

Words are repeated and used frequently in a text to indicate their importance or to emphasize a point. As you begin observing the passage, look for repeated words.

- o Be sure to mark the words *body, one, part(s)/members, all/whole,* and *honor.* Also mark references to the senses each in its own special way: maybe by color, maybe by a specific marking; regardless, make sure each one is distinct from the other.
- o Make a list of what you learn about each word.
- o If you want to go deeper, you can do a word study on any of these keywords. Record what you learn.

Transition words help the reader identify contrasts, comparisons, time, terms of conclusion, or purpose. Mark transition words and record what you learn.

- o Contrasts: but, on the contrary, more/less
- o Comparisons: like, as
- o Time: now, then, after
- o Terms of conclusion: for, therefore, finally
- o Purpose: because, so that

Interpret

Reading in different translations is helpful in gaining greater insight into the meaning of the passage. Read this passage in *The Message* and record any new insights you have as a result.

Look back at your list on the word *body*. You recorded what you learned about the body as it relates to the church in a list. Looking back over that list, what do you learn about God's design for community?

Apply/Engage

As our bodies cease to function when one part isn't working, so it is with our communities. We all have different God-given gifts that help make our communities function when we work together.

- o How does this apply to what God is saying about the church body and your role in it?

- o What changes do you need to make in order to function in community as God intended?

It's easy for us to get caught up in focusing or comparing parts of our bodies to others. No one walks around comparing their liver function to another's, so why do we so readily compare our other "parts"?

- o What did God reveal to you in this passage regarding your own body?

- o Are there any changes you need to make in order to appreciate all your parts?

Enabled through Spiritual Practice

There are many benefits in doing life with others. One way is to participate in a small group community. It could take on many different forms, but its purposes remain the same: to intentionally connect you with other believers on a regular basis to challenge, encourage, and support one another in our daily lives. Jesus formed a small group, better known as the 12 disciples, with whom He met regularly, challenged, encouraged, and taught. What steps might God be asking you to take in regard to a small group community?

Some of you may be sweating or have become suddenly nauseated considering being vulnerable, confessing your sins, and inviting others into the process. Being in community doesn't mean you are now required to be fully transparent with everyone you know or meet. That would be overwhelming, draining, and scary. My anxiety just shot through the roof with that thought. Jesus had the larger group of 12, but within that He had three people whom He held closest to Him and trusted with His innermost thoughts. Maybe your goal should be to start with just one. More insight on that tomorrow.

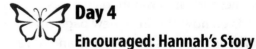

Day 4
Encouraged: Hannah's Story

I knew I needed help. What had started as a strong desire to "be healthy" had turned into a severely restricted diet supplemented by late-night binges and intense, compulsive exercise. Still in high school, my parents kept a close eye on my scattered lifestyle and increasingly harrowed countenance. We had always been close, and I shared at least partially to them about my eating disorder, often at their prompting. Most of the time, I was deep inside my head, unable to see how far I had swung from balance to how sick my mind was. There were times at school where I ate nothing all day. Then I pushed myself after school by running five or six miles.

Food dominated my thoughts, which frustrated me because I knew I was called to set my mind on things above, not on earthly things (Colossians 3:2). I was caught in a cycle of denying myself food all day then losing control at night, then denying myself again all the next day to appease my guilt and make me feel worth it again. I watched my body waste away and felt a sick sense of accomplishment when I looked in the mirror, although improving my appearance wasn't my initial goal, I didn't mind feeling like I had beaten my body into submission and had overcome my own need for food (1 Corinthians 9:27).

One year before, I had sensed the Lord calling me to leave the small Christian middle school I had attended and enroll in the much larger local public high school. I viewed this as the mission field God had assigned to me. While I knew it would be difficult, I didn't expect the depth of the loneliness I would experience. While I battled what I now identify as anorexia, most people who saw me on a daily basis were virtual strangers who didn't know me well enough to call me out on what I was doing. I saw myself as superior and somehow still envied their ability to eat so freely. My isolation had given me the time and space to make me intensely self-focused, which caused me to isolate myself even further.

More painful than my lack of relational depth with other people was my perceived isolation from my Lord, whom I knew would be my only constant in life and in death. It was a season where He seemed silent. I understood the applicable biblical truths: that my body is a temple of the Holy Spirit (1 Corinthians 6:19), that Jesus came so that I could have life to the full (John 10:10), and that my Father would never leave me or forsake me (Joshua 1:5). I knew it all intellectually, but I wanted to know it experientially as well. I kept worshipping Him and living for Him the best I knew how, but I think my struggle with eating is evidence of my attempt to find satisfaction from another source.

It didn't take long for my loving parents to recognize my lifestyle as disordered. With my permission, they put me in touch with a longtime family friend who is a nutrition specialist in a local school district. Opening up to her felt shameful at first, and it took longer than I had hoped to see results. But the Lord used her to show me true compassion: she didn't just take pity on me, but she entered my pain, wrestled in prayer for me, and took my hand to walk with me through a dark night of the soul. She helped me realize my sweet Savior did that for me all my life…He had taken my hand and stood in the fire beside me (Isaiah 41:13).

Coming into the light didn't make my struggle go away immediately. The restriction ran its course and was closely followed by a season of frequent binging, lack of discipline, and rapid weight gain. I was still plagued by the awareness that something was wrong with me. Even now, this fresh new page I'm turning is still stained by the ink of the last one. Every day, I must take up my cross of insecurity and have to fight to believe that what God says about me is enough. His way is the opposite of mine. He tells me to drag into the light ugly things I'd rather stuff in a dark corner, and slowly I'm watching Him make them beautiful. He says I'm at my worst when I feel self-sufficient, and I'm listening as He sings of a love I could never earn. He reminds me to be honest when I feel like plastering on a fake smile, and as I do, I'm receiving the truth that He, the King of the Universe, thinks I'm worth dying for. He declares that I have everything when I surrender all to Him, and I'm prompted to acknowledge His Lordship over every aspect of my life. He shows me that my secret sins die when I bring them out into the open, when I am honest with Him and with the people around me. Little by little, He's teaching me to believe that when I am weak, then I am strong with His power.

Engage

o   How has isolation or difficulty in community affected your eating and body image struggles?

o   What parts of Hannah's story resonated with you, and what will you do as a result?

Enabled through Spiritual Practice

Since we were not designed to walk through our struggles in isolation, I challenge you to find an accountability partner—a trusted friend with whom you can be vulnerable, transparent, honest, and open. Because humans are sinful and at various stages of maturity, be careful to share with someone trustworthy. Ask God to help you find someone who won't condemn you, who will maintain confidentiality, who doesn't press you for more details, and who accepts you as you are. They should be someone who will also lovingly point out your blind spots, challenge the lies you are believing, and walk beside you through the valleys.

Ask the Lord to help you identify that person and then invite them to journey with you. After you set up some meeting guidelines, begin by sharing your stories with one another and pray for each other. As you confess your struggles to each other, you expose the darkness to light and then can stand together against it. As our time of study together comes to a close, an accountability partner can give you much needed support as you continue on your recovery path.

What are some of the characteristics of a person with whom you would entrust your story? List the characteristics that make a person safe to tell. Do you have a person like that in your life? Maybe there is someone in your Transformed group, your Bible study, a person from your church? Begin to pray and ask God to help you find someone.

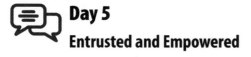 **Day 5**
Entrusted and Empowered

God has put an infrastructure in place through community to help you weather the storms of adversity. Take comfort in knowing that you don't have to go through your struggle alone or isolated. The enemy keeps us stuck in secrecy and shame, believing that we will be condemned if we share our struggles. I found that my burden did feel lighter once I shared it with someone else. Talking about it didn't make it go away, but it did make it lose some of its power over me. Also, when I had others praying for me and walking with me, it made me feel loved and connected and gave me a reason to keep going.

Sharing your struggle with others can also be a blessing to them. God does not waste our suffering, and He often gives us opportunities to walk alongside someone else who is struggling with the same situation. Recovery can often be long and arduous. When I was struggling, every time I met someone who had overcome their eating disorder brought me hope to a seemingly hopeless situation. Now that God has helped me overcome my eating disorder, I can offer hope to those who are struggling just like I was. I used to plead with God to redeem my story by using it to help someone else. I pray that it has helped you.

You don't have to be fully healed in order to share your story. I may be further down the line in my eating disorder recovery, but God is still rooting out the dark areas of my heart, teaching me how to follow Him, and growing my faith through trials. My story is not over yet, but I can share with you as far as I have come and the wisdom that I have gained through my journey. That is all God is asking you to do too. Just share where you are and where you've been. Just being able to say "me too," regardless of where you are in your recovery, offers support and encouragement.

I was so afraid to be vulnerable and share my story, but every time I do, not only do I feel a little freer, but people are more willing to be vulnerable with me. Think of it this way, if you came over to my house, would you feel more comfortable if everything was perfectly kept or if it looked like I actually lived there and didn't have it all together? I know I would choose the latter. It's the same with vulnerability. When you show the other person that you don't have it all together, that you've made mistakes, that you've questioned God and struggled to get through your days, protective walls come down and fear melts away. They no longer fear judgment, condemnation, rejection, or abandonment from you and instead feel safe, heard, understood, and that they can trust you with their hearts.

We have access to so much information today, but in biblical times they relied on the oral tradition to teach, guide, and train up the next generation in the ways of God. God outlines a model for how to do this in Titus 2. A modern-day description of this tradition is mentoring. Mentoring is also a part of God's design for community. We can all benefit from having someone who is a few years ahead of us speak into our lives or someone who has lived through a similar struggle to help us navigate our difficult path. Likewise, we can speak into the lives of someone a few years behind us in age or in their recovery path. We don't have to have life all figured out or our lives put together to do this. This is a come-as-you-are job. God will help us and guide us each step of the way. Most of the time our job is simply to point our mentee back to Him. Not only is it a blessing to her but also to you. God can bring new layers of healing and redemption to your pain as you help someone else. Don't let fear keep you. You've got a story to tell so go out and tell it!

Engage

o   Are there any roadblocks keeping you from sharing your story with others? Ask God what you need to do to remove them.

o   Begin praying that God would raise up someone who could mentor you and someone whom you could mentor. Record what you hear and indicate any action steps God is asking you to take.

Enabled through Spiritual Practice

You learned from the Scripture passage that God has designed each of us with specific gifts and talents that allow us to help each other. Take a few moments to write down a few things that you do well. Then brainstorm different ways you could put those gifts into action to serve others. Maybe you have the gift of hospitality and you could invite some people over from church. Maybe you have the gift of encouragement and you could write a note to your child's teacher. Maybe you are a good cook and could make a double batch of food to bless someone else with a meal. Write down your action plan for the week and step out in faith towards the blessings that await you.

Engage: Final Reflection

Thank you for going on this journey with me. I pray that God has done and will continue to do a transformative work in your heart, mind, and life. I want to challenge you to try doing the mirror exercise again from Session 1. Look at your body again and invite God into the conversation. How has your view changed? Are you able to see yourself through new lenses of love, truth, contentment, trust, humility, grace, forgiveness, and honor? What is God saying to you now, and what do you want to write on your heart anew?

Take some time to sit down and reflect on what you have learned. Start with the introduction by reviewing all of the E-words we used each week and how God used them to connect you with Him. Page through each session and remember some of your aha moments and write down your takeaways. Review the Scripture passages and highlight any instructions the Lord gave you. Note the spiritual disciplines that were most effective in helping you turn to God in the everyday moments. Think about how your view of yourself and of others has changed. Thank God for the ways He has moved and worked in your heart. May you continue to seek Him on this journey.

You have been working hard each week, turning over to God lies you believe, your fears, your discontentment, your idols, your pursuit of perfection, your people pleasing, your pride, your self-imposed rules, your shame, your bitterness, your tendencies to isolate. It is not a process for the faint of heart! It's time to celebrate what the Lord has done! Whether you celebrate often, or this is your first time, hang some streamers, put on some party hats, call up your family and friends, and celebrate this spiritual milestone in your life. Sharing what God has done in your life will not only bless you but will also bless all who hear your testimony. I encourage you to prioritize celebrating God frequently for His work in you. May the blessings abound!

If this Bible study has been transformative in your life, please consider sending in a brief written or video testimony at jennifersmithlane.com to encourage others to do the study as well.

ENDNOTES

1   Holy Bible: The International Standard Version (The ISV Foundation: 2011).

TRANSFORMED – EATING AND BODY IMAGE RENEWAL GOD'S WAY

How-To Guide for Inductive Study

As you read through each Scripture passage each week, you will be walking through a four-step process of prayer, observation, interpretation, and application. (A quick reference guide of the inductive study tools for each section is included at the end of this section.)

Step 1: Prayer

Prayer is an essential first step in your study time. Hebrews 4:12 says, *"For the word of God is alive and powerful. It is sharper than the sharpest two-edged sword, cutting between soul and spirit, between joint and marrow. It exposes our innermost thoughts and desires"* (NLT). Scripture cannot do this work in you unless you invite the Holy Spirit to teach you as you study.

Step 2: Observation

Observation is essentially a process of investigating the facts in order to lead to a more accurate understanding of Scripture. As you work through the different tools, develop a marking system that works for you. For example, in my own study, I find it helpful to mark what I observe in the same color or fashion, so that repeated words, places, expressions of time, imperatives, main characters, and the like visually stand out on the page. Once you formulate your own marking style, make a list on a 3x5 card or in the margin so that you can be consistent throughout the passage. Some people like to use colored pencils, some don't. Some like to use different shapes, some don't. Don't get hung up on this. There is no right or wrong way to do it, so do what works for you.

Step 3: Interpretation

Interpretation is the process of taking the facts you've learned a step further by discovering what it means. Careful consideration of the context of the passage and cross references will help you determine the meaning of the passage. While there are different human authors to each book, God is truly the author of all Scripture. Therefore, Scripture cannot contradict itself. If a contradiction arises, likely your interpretation needs refining.

Step 4: Application

Once you have thoroughly completed steps 1-3, you are ready to apply what you learned to your own life. The spiritual disciplines section helps you employ these changes by teaching you practical tools you can use in your everyday life.

Feeling overwhelmed? I felt the same way too the first time I tried this method. Know that your efforts will not be in vain, because God promises that His Word will not return to Him empty (Isaiah 55:11). Have courage, beloved, and give it a try.

Helpful Resources
For a more in-depth explanation and resources for inductive study visit precept.org.

Tools for Studying Scripture

Always use **Scripture** as the source text for your study.

THE METHOD:

Prayer, Observation, Interpretation, Application

1. **PRAYER** (The **Holy Spirit** is the teacher. **He** is **TRUTH** and will guide you into all truth, John 16:32)

2. **OBSERVATION** (What does the text say? What do I see?)
   o   Read and Re-read for an **Overview** of the entire book
   o   Look for **Main Characters** (references to **God**, to **author**, to **recipients**)
   o   Ask **5W's and H** (who, what, where, when, why, how)
   o   Look at **Context** (what precedes and what follows the text)
   o   Look for **Repeated Key Words or Phrases**
   o   Look for **Lists** (simple, topical)
   o   Look for **Contrasts** (but)
   o   Look for **Comparisons** (using words "like" and "as")
   o   Look for **Terms of Conclusion** ("therefore," "finally," "in conclusion")
   o   Look for **Expressions of "Time"**
   o   Look for **Instructions, Commands, Exhortations**

3. **INTERPRETATION** (What does it mean?)
   o   Compare Scripture with Scripture (**Cross References**). Remember context rules and Scripture can never contradict Scripture.
   o   Ask the **5 W's and H** questions (For interpretation – e.g., Why did Jesus say it that way?)
   o   **Ask** what is the "therefore" there for?
   o   Do **word study** using a dictionary, concordance, and other tools

4. **APPLICATION** (How does the truth in this text apply to my life?)
   o   **Living out God's Truth** that was shown to me and **Producing Good Fruit**
   o   **Being Transformed** into the **Likeness of Christ**

Questions and Answers

What if I don't know Jesus Christ?

If you would like to know more about having a saving and personal relationship with Jesus Christ, there is no time like the present! We are by nature sinners, and our sin separates us from God. The good news is that God sent His Son, Jesus, to die on a cross for our sins to bridge the gap between us and God. By accepting Jesus as our Lord and Savior, we renounce our life of sin and receive eternal and abundant life with God.

Ready to embark on a life with Jesus? Start by praying this prayer. *Lord, I need You. I confess the sinful things I have done. Thank You for forgiving me of my sins. I believe that You died on the cross for me and rose again. I desire to dedicate my life to You and I am asking You to come into my life and reign in my heart as my Savior. Transform me into the person You designed me to be. Thank You, God. In Jesus' name I pray, amen.*

If you just prayed this prayer, hallelujah! Your sins have been washed clean by the blood of Jesus, and I welcome you warmly to the body of Christ! The next step is to tell another believer in your life or contact your local church about how to grow and nurture your faith.

What materials do I need to get started?

- o   Bible
- o   Journal for reflection questions (optional)
- o   Colored pencils/pens for marking text (optional)

What is inductive Bible study?

It is a method that helps you to discover God's truth in your own personal study of Scripture using a four-step process of prayer, observation, interpretation, and application, instead of relying on others to tell you what it means.

What other resources are available to help me with the inductive study method?

- o   Precept Ministries (precept.org)
- o   Blueletterbible.org
- o   Living by the Book by Howard Hendricks
- o   Dictionary and Bible Concordance
- o   jennifersmithlane.com/resources

What are spiritual disciplines?

They are practices used to develop and deepen our spiritual maturity using methods Christians have employed for centuries. They help us transform our desires for a more vibrant prayer life, for a deeper connection to God, into a reality through the practice of both inward and outward activities. These methods are designed to help all explore and experience the spiritual realm in a more intimate way.

Appendix

Can I do this study alone or should I do it with a group?

The study is designed so that it can be used in both settings. While doing the study by yourself is a worthy endeavor, doing it with someone else or in a group can only enhance your experience. A group setting is helpful for not feeling alone in your struggle, accountability, and encouragement. Prayerfully consider which format is best for you.

What are the different kinds of eating disorders?

- *Anorexia nervosa:* excessive weight loss through restricting food intake
- *Anorexia Athletica:* (Hypergymnasia) excessive and compulsive exercise
- *Bulimia nervosa:* eating excessive amounts of food followed by purging behaviors
- *Binge Eating:* eating excessive amounts of food
- *Orthorexia:* excessive preoccupation with eating healthy food
- *Emotional Eating:* eating to numb emotions
- *Extreme Dieting:* excessive dieting that pushes your body beyond healthy limits
- *Obesity:* excessively overweight resulting in health problems
- *Body Dissatisfaction:* negative thoughts and feelings around body size and shape
- *EDNOS:* (Eating Disorder Not Otherwise Specified): combination of those listed above

What if I don't have an eating disorder; is this study right for me?

You don't have to have an official eating disorder diagnosis to struggle with disordered eating or with body dissatisfaction. While the study is designed specifically for women struggling with eating and body image issues, the underlying areas addressed apply to situations far beyond this area. I would encourage you to give it a try.

Resources

Inductive Method

- o   Kay Arthur, *How to Study Your Bible: The Lasting Rewards of the Inductive Method*
- o   Howard G. Hendricks and William D. Hendricks, *Living by the Book: The Art and Science of Reading the Bible*

Spiritual Disciplines

- o   Adele Ahlberg Calhoun, *Spiritual Disciplines Handbook; Practices That Transform Us*
- o   Richard J. Foster, *Celebration of Discipline: The Path to Spiritual Growth*

Eating Disorders

- o   www.nationaleatingdisorders.org
- o   www.mieda.org

Difficult Relationships

- o   Leslie Vernick, *The Emotionally Destructive Relationship: Seeing It, Stopping It, Surviving It*
- o   Dr. Henry Cloud & Dr. John Townsend, *Boundaries: When to Say Yes, How to Say No to Take Control of Your Life*

More Resources available at jennifersmithlane.com/resources

Tips for Group Leaders

Pray: Pray for your participants, for their needs, for their transformation, for the leaders, for protection. Establish a prayer team who can cover you and your group for the duration of the study.

Prepare: Prayerfully invite participants and determine when, where, and how long you will meet. Plan an introductory meeting to go over the materials and get to know each other.

Set Up: Create a comfortable physical environment by making the space inviting; a safe emotional environment by emphasizing confidentiality; and a protected spiritual environment by praying through the space beforehand.

Facilitate: Be trustworthy, transparent, timely, prayerful, encouraging, and quick to listen. Create opportunities for all to share, set boundaries, promote God-focused discussion and avoid possible triggering food/weight specifics.

Concerns: If a participant's mental or physical health is in danger, assist them in seeking professional help immediately.

Equip: Find more resources for leaders at jennifersmithlane.com.

Printed in the USA
CPSIA information can be obtained
at www.ICGtesting.com
LVHW080145051023
759988LV00020B/1627